CW01498366

The Hippie Trail 1974

Dover to Delhi the hard way -
by Coach, Bus and Train!

Simon Sharpe

Printed edition 2023
Publisher: Hillfort Books, England
hillfortbooks@gmail.com
ISBN: 978-1-8383239-2-9

Dedicated to all travellers and wanderers of the earth.

Contents

INTRODUCTION

Different kinds of young people from Western Europe, North America and even Australia travelled the 'hippie trail' from Europe to India or Kathmandu in Nepal in the 1950s to the 70s. That long land route from Europe to India that included part of the ancient Silk Road. If you were Australian, you did it in reverse. However, from 1979 that journey could no longer be safely made as the politics of the Islamic countries we had travelled through changed. Indeed, for any young westerner who was not a Muslim to try it today would be to invite disappearance, imprisonment and perhaps an early death.

Yet in those days the politics of post-war Europe meant we had to travel through the secretive Iron Curtain communist countries of Yugoslavia or Bulgaria first, for the real journey East began once Europe was passed and our feet were firmly in Istanbul in exotic Turkey. Still to sample would be Iran, experiencing a modern economy under the rulership of the Shah. Then the mysteriousness of Afghanistan, which would be the final destination of many of the hippie travellers for whom the appeal of the hippie trail was found growing in the village fields of that country. And if you were Brits you hoped for a welcome in our former Empire territories that made up Pakistan and India.

I had no camera. Couldn't afford one and I never saw a hippie with one on the trail. But I was a traveller on the trail, not a tourist or a hippie and I was determined to do the trip again as a tourist, with a camera when I had a bit more cash and could travel in a lot more comfort.

Even without a camera I still wanted to remember the details of this journey, and a year after my return I took a cassette tape recorder and filled three hours as I talked myself through my travels, remembering the events and characters of the journey through the items I had collected on the way and a journey notebook. Then the passage of life overtook me; study, work, career, marriage, kids, new career, house moves, etc. Finally in 2020 the Covid pandemic arrived in England and life for millions of us came to a sudden halt. Lockdown now gave many of us the opportunity to explore the dark recesses of our homes and rediscover life's baggage of many years hidden there; and for me these tapes.

With no camera, I had nevertheless kept coach, bus and train tickets and travel docs and bank slips. And the smell of them recently, as I took them out of the leather pouch I had used as a secure place for my money (around my neck) instantly took me back to the trail nearly fifty years ago. A mixed aroma of sweat, leather and paper documents baked in 120°F of heat, and the dust of hot lands and deserts. Oh, the power of smell to trigger memories! And the passport stamps were great souvenirs too; evidence almost as good as a selfie.

I had better tell you now that this is not a tale of meeting drug dealers in Middle Eastern back alleys or of days spent in a cannabis coma or opium haze. There was no judgement on that. I had seen alcohol destroy many people's lives and that drug was quite legal to buy and enjoy. Mine was and still is a body that cannot cope with the smallest drop of alcohol, never mind any hippie narcotic and, as you will find out, the heat of the summer on the trail nearly killed me. I was unprepared in so many ways. But I had twelve weeks of freedom that summer before college began in September, and travel on the hippie trail was an intoxicating thought too great to miss.

The world that we know now was not always this way. The Middle East didn't always hate westerners. Before Tony Blair and George W. Bush and their wars in Iraq and

Afghanistan, or John Major and George Bush (snr) in Iraq and Kuwait, or the Russians in Kabul and Islamic fundamentalism widespread, there was a peaceful relationship between governments of nations of admittedly different cultures and economic success, but a Middle East that tolerated difference and whose culture welcomed strangers.

In the eighteenth century, the Grand Tour of Europe and its capital cities, ancient monuments and museums was the delight of wealthy English men and women. The adventurers of Victorian Britain explored further taking an army and trade and missionaries to all parts of the globe. The two World Wars of the twentieth century broadened the world experience of another generation - our parent's generation.

British politicians that came after the Second World War didn't want another war. By the 1960s the consensus was that they wanted a united Europe, a United Nations, UNESCO, peace, social justice, equality and freedom. Reluctantly or not, Britain gave up its colonies while Parliament saw through, under the Labour government, the Abortion Law Reform Act, began the decriminalization of homosexuality and finally killed-off capital punishment.

There was, in the UK, the growth in public services like the National Health Service, housing projects, social work, prison reform, state pensions, comprehensive and free university education. These values were also expressed through the growth of charities like Oxfam, Amnesty International, Save the Children, Shelter and many others.

Nevertheless, the personal freedom of the youth born post World War Two needed something else. For the generation that grew up after the war there was a pulling at social bonds and constraints within the home and social norms were changing for so many.

Popular music brought popular culture with its own fashions, films, language and ultimately values. The ordinary people of Britain, the parents of these 'teenagers', felt their traditional values and those of previous generations threatened. They didn't understand their youth.

Elvis Presley, as early as 1956, was giving the youth of America the opportunity for self-exploration and the parents feared that kids would begin to question their own way of life. Rock and Roll music was seen as a highway to rebellion and particularly white America called it the 'devil's music'. A gap was growing between teens and their parents.

The growth of young people driving cars allowed for sex outside of hotels and marriage, and ample opportunity for what you were not meant to do, as Jerry Lee Lewis reminded us in *Wake-up Little Susie!*. Or as Brian Wilson and the Beach Boys sang,

'She'll have fun, fun, fun 'till her Daddy takes the T-Bird away'.

Music and films aimed particularly at youth, harnessed a power and a language that challenged social norms, and full employment meant money that gave teens the freedom to make life choices of their own. Marlo Brando, in the 1950s, asked the question for this post war generation in the film *The Wild Ones*; 'What are *you* rebelling against?' It was easier to know what you were rebelling against than exactly what you were hoping to find.

In the 1960s, '*Switch on, tune in, drop out*' was the call of the counter-culture priest Timothy Leary from San Francisco. The word 'hippie' from that period was replacing 'beatnik', and was said to describe someone who had decided to;

free themselves from societal restrictions and choose their own way, and find new meaning in life, such as acceptance of recreational drug use, liberal sexual mores, advocacy of communal living and a strong pacifism or anti-war sentiment.

One expression of hippie independence was their standard of dress, mainly jeans, tee-shirts, peace and love emblems, often an ethnic look, and grooming, which for men meant long hair and beards, and this made hippies instantly recognizable to one another. Hippies declared their willingness to question authority. Mysticism, honesty, non-violence and joy were values they claimed.

In the UK with full employment and money to spare, youth, whether hippies or not, found the relatively mild recreational drugs of cannabis and marijuana to their taste. However, because such things were not just seen as antisocial but illegal, many decided to travel to the source of them where they had heard it was cheap and legal to enjoy, and where eastern religions might enhance their own spiritual search to fill any emptiness within.

For some, as travel became cheaper and easier, there was the motivation and opportunity to explore further than your own backyard. The Liverpool Beatles found it in 1968 in meditation in India without the need to use the well-established hippie trail. What could the average young westerner do? Answer: Go and find these things for themselves. The world was our oyster - although for some it could become a nipping lobster.

So, if you travelled on the trail, what was your motivation? For motivation would guide your experiences. Mine was pure escapism and adventure.

Chapter 1
The Need for Adventure

I had had a set of grandparents who had been adventurers. George, my Dad's dad, had gone to South Africa before the Boer Wars in the late 1890s, working to bring supplies and entertainments to the British troops. George's brother Charles, my great-uncle, was killed there at the siege of Mafeking when a Boer shell destroyed his shop premises with him in it.

My Dad's mother had been born in India where her father Alfred had been stationed as a sergeant in the Horse Artillery. Alfred, they said, had served in India at the time of the Indian Mutiny of 1857, when the Indian sepoys led an insurrection against the many injustices they felt they, and the Indian people, were subjected to by the British.

Alfred's young wife, Sarah, then sailed out to join him aged twenty-two, on a troopship calling at the garrison

towns and staging posts at Gibraltar, Malta, St. Helena, Cape Town, Port Elizabeth, Bombay and so to Calcutta. Then she was pulled on a barge by relays of Indians up the Hoogly and Ganges rivers to the garrison town of Cawnpore, now called Canpur.

Sarah, as a young bride, was lucky to miss the first battle of Cawnpore in June 1857 when the British had to surrender and were then massacred by the mutineers, including all the women and children. She was in Cawnpore for the second Battle in the following December, when General Campbell routed 25,000 rebels for the loss of only 99 British soldiers.

Sarah's daughter, my grandmother Maud, had travelled from England to South Africa by ship in 1904 as a teacher of music and scripture to army children. George and Maud had married in 1906 in Bloemfontein cathedral, and we had photos of her in a long dress on a horse with the primitive corrugated iron-roofed houses of the new township as a backdrop.

By contrast I was born in a Dorset cottage at the end of a mile-long drove, an outpost of a village that had disappeared in a plague in the 1500s, and had left isolated farms and a church in a field as communities that had escaped and survived. My Dad sold chemicals and animal foodstuffs to Dorset farmers but had itchy feet himself. When his firm opened an office in Nairobi, Dad decided to take us all to East Africa.

There a wonderful man called James Araina, tall, jet black from the Luo tribe close to Lake Victoria and with a huge, warm engaging smile, came into our lives and cooked and cleaned and washed our clothes, while my mother worked for the Red Cross in the highland villages.

Travel to Africa in 1957 was an adventure best undertaken by sea and the 'Warwick Castle' didn't disappoint. Once the British government had angered the Egyptians, who blocked the Suez Canal, we had to go the long way to East Africa via Cape Town. The 'Castles' had been pre-war ocean liners converted to flat-top aircraft carriers for convoy duty in the Second World War.

We called at Las Palmas in the Canaries. As children we hailed the other occasional passing ships and wrote ridiculous notes and stuffed them inside every empty tin and bottle we could find and cast them overboard in the hope they might be found. (Of course, they lie untouched at the bottom of the Atlantic and Indian oceans.)

Flying fish would surface and scoot across the waves at the prow of the ship as we reached warmer waters, and a school of dolphins, or were they porpoises, would be seen by someone and then a call would go out and all would line the rails and gaze at these creatures, as curious of our activities as we were of theirs. As we crossed the Equator we were covered in cream and dunked in the First-Class passengers' swimming pool by the Chief Petty Officer acting as Neptune.

Then on through the tropics, burning ourselves in blazing heat in the canvas pool rigged up on deck for the Third-Class passengers. These were mainly the wives and children joining husbands and fathers already arrived in their part of Africa by air.

We woke up early one morning to an eerie stillness in the ship; we were at anchor. Then the bustling and laughter in the corridors and calls to go on deck. And when we did, we saw one of the world's great sights; Cape Town with Table Mountain from the bay. A quick stop, we were told, and if we went ashore we had to be back at the ship by 4pm. Could we get up Table Mountain in that time?

A motor-launch was made ready and with other families we scrambled in. At the dockside found a taxi to take us to the landing stage for the cable car ride. But already grey clouds were forming and before we had gone very far our driver stopped the car and pointed. A cap of mist now enveloped the mountain. Or rather, a grey fluffy tablecloth covered and hung down its sides. There was no sign of the cable car. We took the taxi back to the harbour.

Durban and the old Portuguese port of Beira passed before we saw surf crashing on a reef, as we made our way past the crowded island of Mombasa and docked at the grey and whitewashed featureless port. But the smell! Another unforgettable smell, this time of tropical heat on sand and warm seas and the rotting vegetation of the palm forest on the mainland.

That evening we travelled by train across 300 miles of the African plains to Nairobi where our Dad met us. Then, in his brand-new Peugeot 303, we drove down the escarpment road and the 97 miles to the little town of Nakuru. The escarpment road had been built by Italian prisoners of war and with a perilous drop to our left we could look into the Great Rift Valley floor a thousand feet below and see, sixty miles away, the peak of the extinct volcano called Longonot. This great valley, the cradle of ancient humanity over millions of years, was to be our home for the next five.

Nakuru, was a town built by the railroad fifty years before and divided geographically by the three skin colours of its residents, black, brown and white; African, Indian and European. These characteristics determined where you lived, what education you received, how you worked and which hospital you could die in. Nobody called it 'apartheid'.

We lived in a large bungalow built of breeze blocks at the beginning of the century set in acres of grounds. I had my first air pistol at nine and an air rifle at ten. But we called the police to shoot the python that had hidden in Dad's car engine after he had parked in long grass on a farm. It foolishly revealed itself when he put the car back home in the car port. My mother regretted not asking for the skin to make some shoes or a handbag.

We kept pet chameleons and watched them snatch flies with their long sticky tongues; made rafts out of drums and planks to float on Lake Nakuru watched by a million flamingo; we took our bikes up on top of Mt. Menengai and investigated the caldera of the world's third largest extinct volcano, to count the number of smoke trails rising from the forest floor below.

One Christmas, we rode the surf at Mombasa and fished from the reef in dug-out canoes. Other times we stayed at the Silverbeck Hotel at Nanyuki, close to Mt Kenya, placed so accurately that the Equator line ran through the bar. We went horse riding on the lower slopes of the mountain with a trail of thirty dogs to keep the lions at bay. For a day out we could tour the game parks. We travelled one hundred miles just to see '*Snow White and the Seven Dwarfs*' on the silver screen at an airless Nairobi cinema.

The most exciting thing we had done in England was huddle on the beach at Weston-Super-Mare or Bournemouth with our sandwiches, waiting for the tide to venture in. Or in winter, take a toboggan and slide down the snowy

slopes of the ancient hillfort at Badbury Rings, in the days before global warming robbed children of that pleasure.

By 1960 travel back to England for a six-week holiday was by propeller driven Viscount or Britannia aircraft. They made all the stops, dropping off and picking up government officials and businessmen, a few tourists; Entebbe, Addis Abba, Khartoum, Benghazi, Paris or Rome and finally, twenty-four long hours later, a rain-soaked Heathrow. Now it is an eight-hour non-stop joyless flight.

As Kenya headed for independence and Europeans in isolated farms were being murdered by a resurgent freedom movement, we flew back to England. From our large bungalow set in some acres, we came back to live in a Victorian bay-windowed terrace house in a Bristol side street with a postage stamp back garden. Most families in the UK still didn't possess a car, which had been essential for life in Africa. Life in the UK was not just physically restricting. It was socially incomprehensible to me and my brother.

Even at weekends kids still dressed in school uniforms as they had nothing else to wear. Cousin Tim had enjoyed a week's holiday at Brean Sands - but he only lived 40 miles away in Bristol. My brother raised his eyebrows and quipped, 'Big safari!' Life was so small. This island - so overcrowded.

There was just nowhere to shoot a gun, nowhere interesting to ride to on a bike, and there was a strict expectation of social behaviour that, as wild colonial boys, my brother and I completely lacked. School uniform was with ties, and caps which you raised if you saw someone you knew. Kenyan life was casual.

Neighbours here were only a few feet away, not a hundred yards, and you blew your nose each night to get the day's smog and pollution out of your system. You took a mackintosh coat with you every time you left home, because the chances were it would rain before you returned.

Britain – was the place we called 'home' in East Africa and longed for the day of our return to the new youth and pop culture of the 1960s. Confusingly we found it was full of gossipy neighbours, grumpy old people mostly born in the Victorian era and wrapped in grey or brown overcoats with hats or scarves on their heads; and for the men, always a cigarette or pipe in their hand or mouth.

And why were there so many old people? They were everywhere; millions of grey-haired, thin old people (and there was no obesity in those times). I was shocked. My mother explained. 'Africa and the colonies have always taken the youth of Britain to govern and defend it', she said. 'That's why you never saw British people out there over fifty, except the few original settlers. When they got old, people came back 'home' to Britain.'

Buildings were caked in black soot from a thousand chimneys, and rooms and adult fingers were stained with nicotine. Cigarette smoke at least concealed the smell of body odour. Every house smelt of moth balls and coal gas.

In winter you cleared the ice off the *inside* of your bedroom windows and waited until someone had lit a real fire in one room. Then, we would quickly leap out of bed and drag our clothes in there to dress. We had to learn the lessons of fire-lighting; first the coiled paper, then the sticks of wood and then the coal.

Gardens were tiny, shops expensive, green buses took everyone everywhere. We had never been on a bus before. It drizzled most days and the first winter of 1962, we were snowed in for a week. 'Oh God, get me out of here', was my cry that never seemed to be answered.

Here it was not the colour of your skin that determined the course of your life and your life chances. Social class determined where you lived, your school and who you spoke to, what you wore and how you talked and where you shopped. Africa was freedom and not just wide-open skies.

England was going to choke the life out of me.

One day on busy Park Street, I came across the window of an art shop that completely expressed my feelings about my life here. Displayed was a David Shepherd oil painting of lions resting under a thorn tree from the heat of the blue African skies, with open savannah behind to distant mountains beyond. Next to it, an L.S. Lowrie of smoking chimneys and thin, impoverished figures hurtling along a grimy street of smoking factories, somewhere in the north of England, beneath dark lowering skies.

By 1974 I was twenty-four and still hadn't settled for the social constraints of England. I had spent a year running a homeless hostel and seen the damage that alcohol, meths and rough cider could do in the hands of elderly veterans of two World Wars, and drugs to the youth of Britain. I was also a qualified teacher that had realized that to be locked in a building with hundreds of kids was never going to give me the adventure I craved. I was heading for a few years in social work.

I had met Tricia a couple of years before my trip. Tall, dark, bright and animated, this university graduate was into social protest and was an active member of Child Poverty Action Group. She had helped on our soup runs for the homeless. Flowered long skirts, blouses and jackets, she spoke of having been on the hippie trail the year before. Tricia and her boyfriend had travelled to India on his motor bike, she said. It had broken down somewhere in rural north India on their way to Kathmandu. They had sought help in a village.

'A Hindu family from the village took us in,' she said, 'and gave us shelter in a back room of their hut, for the night. They had no electricity or running water...not that it mattered. But we drank their water and got dysentery. We couldn't do anything for two weeks, except crawl out to the fields to be sick or for a shit and try and drink the chai they offered.'

For the 9 months prior to my departure to India I had been working in a book distribution centre in Bristol. Finding the books in the warehouse and packing them off to shops. I was the dispatch clerk.

One morning the manager came to me with a pallet load of boxes of children's educational literature. Each month, he wanted me to fill a large post office sack of these boxes to send to a Christian missionary organization in Bombay, now Mumbai. These sacks were famously made by serving prisoners and faithfully had eight stitches to the inch around the side. My job was then to weigh the bag, secure it and ensure the luggage label was filled in and signed by me, or customs would send it back.

The bags started a conversation with tall, lean, graduate in History, Harold one morning at the coffee machine. It was obvious we were both overqualified for the jobs we were doing in the warehouse.

'I was in India last year,' I heard him say as the 70s hot drinks machine frothed and spat 'white coffee with sugar' for him.

'Did you fly? You must have money,' I quipped.

'No, the hippie trail.' Harold was a man of
few words.

'Did you do it for the drugs?' I ventured.

'Most people do,' he said, 'but a good number just want to travel far and cheaply, see the sights, find a bit of freedom away from the shackles of home.'

'Sounds like what I need,' I mused aloud; my curiosity was sparking into life. 'How did you travel?' I had to ask.

His coffee was too hot to drink; the conversation extended. 'I had a couple of friends, and we booked a coach to take us all the way to Kathmandu. It picked up a load of us in London. We got quickly through Europe. Don't want to spend too long there, too expensive.' Harold sipped at his coffee and winced.

'What did it cost you?'

He mentioned a figure which to my disappointment was beyond my reach working in the warehouse at £16.00 per week. Then he added, 'What takes you furthest on the least money, is doing it all by local transport, bus and train.'

'What - seriously? Where do you stay if you don't have a coach to sleep in?'

'Well, you don't sleep in the coach unless you really must. There's plenty of cheap hotels to use everywhere. Most people go as far as their money takes them, or half their money anyway,' my friend said. 'Leave enough to get back. Get a copy of Private Eye, you'll find all the adverts for travel in the back of that.'

Private Eye, that satirical magazine that took the piss out of the politicians and encouraged you to look at life from a different angle. I got one on the way home. Harold was right, it was all there. All the options.

I thought I would be clever and booked a return coach trip from London to Istanbul. That way if I was skint in Istanbul on the return I could still get home. Need I worry? The world, and specifically the Middle East, was at peace. Nothing could possibly go wrong... could it? The world was my oyster. And all over the world, the British passport was the top trump card for travellers. To travel throughout Europe, and then from Turkey to India, the only visa I would need to buy would be for Afghanistan.

Leave Old England behind and find life and adventure. Oh yes, that was for me! I always wondered if I would ever get as far as India. Maybe I might only get to Turkey or Iran or Afghanistan. I had hoped on my small amount of money and the few weeks I had for the trip, to touch Delhi. I know many went further to Nepal, but time and money were my limitations.

I had some savings which I didn't want to touch, yet. From my meagre earnings of £16.00 per week, six pounds was rent for my room at the YMCA. When I finally left for India, I had some English cash, £64.60 in Travellers cheques (worth about £600.00 now) and an open-return ticket to and from Istanbul with a bus company called Magic Bus, who had advertised themselves in Private Eye, Oz and one or two other 'underground' magazines.

The ticket cost £45.00 and while they were not mainstream, nothing was that was going to Turkey at that time. I didn't think in my three months away that much would happen to disturb a successful return journey later in the summer. I was in a hurry. Planning? I should have done more! I made too many assumptions. But, heck, in twelve weeks or less I should be back home.

I travelled alone. I hadn't meant to. On the warehouse floor I had met Peter who at twenty-six was living the kind of aimless life that could not be enjoyed, and in reality was searching for a secure job or a career in something, but he wasn't sure what. With nothing else on his horizon, he said he would come.

As I was planning to set us both up with coach tickets to Istanbul, he told me our adventure was not to be. His application for a desk career in the mighty Post Office had been accepted. This was such a contrast to the adventure we had planned that it came as something of a shock. Alone I must do it. June was approaching and time was getting tight if I was to be back in the UK by September.

Chapter 2
Magic Bus

I took with me a red, nylon, aluminium framed rucksack. It was packed with food, thin summer clothes and other things I thought I would need including a very small one-man tent. I had heard that many hotels on the journey allowed camping in their gardens, and although Harold had told me about the hotels, I hadn't realized just how cheap they were to be.

Some information about travelling overland to India was obtained from booklets advertised in Private Eye and other youth press that circulated around universities and colleges throughout Europe. The advice there in was explic-

it about which hotels to stay in, which had bugs or were expensive and which bus companies to use. They also gave advice on where to get Student Cards so that you could travel, not just in Turkey but throughout Europe and Asia, much more cheaply. As I travelled I wished I had read more of them.

The night before my departure I stayed with Harold in north London, and on Saturday 8th June 1974 I took the Underground to Victoria Station for 9.30am where I was to meet up with other travellers on the mysteriously named 'Magic Bus'. Magic Bus gave their address as 27 Giesbach

Road, London N19 and said they had an operator in Hotel Gungor at Sultanahmet in Istanbul from where their bus would return to the UK each Sunday. Jeans, hair and bulging rucksacks, but little evidence of the flower-power peace and love movement here amongst the mainly North American and British travellers. Maybe those emblems had been left back in the 60s. It was summer and students were now at the end of their studies and three months of adventure beckoned for them too. Europe was not the destination for many but simply the route to Istanbul where the true journey to the East would begin.

Outside the Continental Booking Office there was no sign of the Magic Bus operator. Had we been suckers and given our money to something that didn't exist? These lone operators were maybe not the most reliable, and it could mean they had taken our money and run.

Half an hour late, a woman arrived. No flowery-powery idealism about her. This was just business. She told us we would be taking the train to Dover and the ferry across the channel to Ostend where we would pick up the Magic Bus.

We crossed the Channel in rough seas with our escort, but at the Ostend ferry terminal there was no Magic Bus. Flustered, she apologized, and we sheltered from the summer drizzle at a café/bar at the centre of the port. She gave us the Magic Bus business card, and if I had been more awake to life I might have wondered at the inability of the  operator to get the phone number digits on the card in the correct sequence. What else might they get wrong?

We waited and drank Stella, cool and bitter on the

tongue. Darkness descended and we waited some more and then ventured out into the drizzle to buy food for the journey before the shops closed.

Finally, at around 11pm, the Magic Bus arrived. Hooting into the car park swerved the dated and worn two-tone, buff-coloured coach. No decorative Magic Bus logo; no pastel artwork adorned its sides; no 'Peace and Love' emblems decorated its snub-nosed bonnet; no flower motifs brightened the windows; no rock music belched from its speakers. There was nothing 'Magic' about this – until you climbed in and smelt the marijuana and sat on the cramped, ancient and furry seats. This was a trip back in time!

"Sorry, guys and girls, left my glasses in Brussels and had to go back for them," explained a thirty-something bearded Belgium bloke dressed in brown corduroys and beaming to hide his embarrassment. His accent was thick, and brown seemed to be the logo-colour of the Magic Bus. Interesting.

None of this was instilling in me much confidence, yet these were the people I was to depend on to get me back from Istanbul in a few months. Disorganised and neglectful so far; were they bordering on the shambolic? But I was going to learn that the hippie trail was not a place for consistency, continuity or professionalism. It was the place you would learn to 'wing it', tolerate other people's faults, try to avoid 'rip-offs' from sellers and 'hassles' from authorities and to live on your wits.

Your fellow travellers would mean well, as you were all part of that stream of western youth flowing together along the same route with largely the same purpose. To stay safe, you had to stay with the main flow, avoid the rapids, the whirlpools and side eddies and trust to nothing. Whatever experiences you had, good or bad, were all part of the adventure.

No-one I spoke to carried travel insurance. Yes, your

British passport was still the best kind of travel insurance. Surely we Brits were respected in every country we were to pass through, still remembered as the victors of the Second World War. Were we not to be remembered fondly in Pakistan and India as kindly colonialists who had brought them a common language to unify their disparate peoples and a railway system that was the envy of the world? After all, didn't we put the Shah on his throne in Iran in the 1950s? And Turkey? Well, let's forget the Dardanelles in WW1. Ataturk had created a new western-looking state in the 1920s, and most of us travellers had seen the film *Top Kapi* with Peter Ustinov, and the Turks seemed pretty friendly to Europeans in that.

The coach already had pairs of US college students touring Europe and who would disembark at various points as we travelled. The hippie trail was not for many of them. They had already travelled 4,000 miles or more from across the USA or Canada to get to Europe. For most of them, Europe was education and adventure enough.

The food we bought in Ostend proved useful as we never stopped long enough on the 3-day journey to make the changing of money into a local currency, which then was in francs, deutschmarks, drachmas, etc. worthwhile. We appreciate the Euros now.

Heading for Istanbul were Mike and Phil, a tough looking couple of young Aussies whose only luggage was the blue denim suits they stood in and a cache of cash in belts around their waists. They had done labouring jobs in Australia to earn enough money to travel the overland route to England; the hippie trail in reverse. Now they were going back home through Europe. They planned to travel on the trail to India and across to Calcutta and then work their way on a ship to either Singapore or Australia.

Clive was from Rhodesia; this was before the country gained independence as Zimbabwe. However, as his Rhodesian passport was unacceptable in most countries because of the failure of his white government to give the black Africans the vote, he was travelling on an Irish passport through his mother's family line.

Clive's family ran a farm near Bulawayo and treated the black Africans workers very well, he said, but understood that the country would have to go to majority rule eventually. He was trying to avoid the draft into his country's security forces. He was only going as far as his money took him in Europe and he left us in Vienna.

Two quiet Canadians guys spent the journey reading their New Testaments. 'Getting ready for Bible college in September, back home.' They too left us somewhere in Europe.

The journey itself was uneventful. We crossed through Belgium, into Germany overnight and into Austria on the Sunday. With little traffic on the road, we travelled quickly once we had left western Europe, and by Monday we were in communist Yugoslavia, throwing up dust on their main roads still laid with stone and gravel that had served the community for hundreds of years.

The lorries and buses in this country were ancient and few, cars almost none and no tractors on the farms. In the summer fields men were pitchforking hay onto horse-drawn haywains. We stopped outside Zagreb at a street café and I grabbed an omelette and tea. In Greece we stopped for an hour to soak up the heat and sun and enjoy ice-cream and our first sight of the Mediterranean.

Magic Bus had been built for the cooler climate of northern Europe and had no air-conditioning, just portions of the roof that opened up to the skies. An early form of climate control - yup, you had the same climate that was outside the coach, just warmer, on those furry seats!

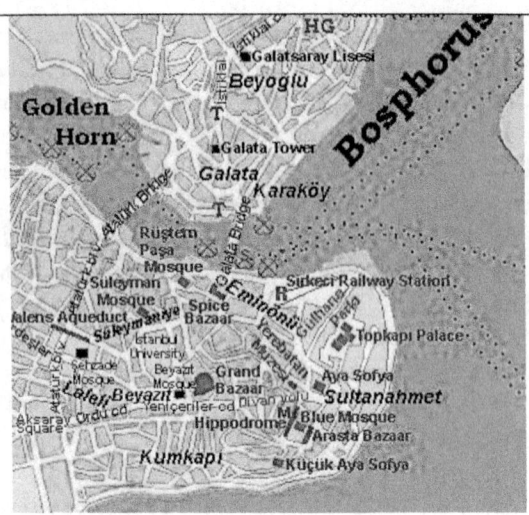

Chapter 3
Istanbul

At 2.20am on Tuesday morning 11th June we woke to find ourselves in Istanbul, parked outside a middling hotel close to the Top Kapi museum opposite the Hagia Sophia Grand Mosque. We slept in the coach till dawn. This was June, high summer, and the daytime temperature in Istanbul was in the eighties and, surrounded on three sides by water, the humidity was high.

The toilets on the hippie trail were the first cultural shock. At least in Istanbul you could sit down rather than squat, but the sewers of old Istanbul couldn't cope with the used paper, so there was a large dustbin beside the toilet for your paperwork. Imagine!

Sultanahmed was an old part of the city. Its busy uphill road had on the right, old buildings three or four stories high that had on the ground floor, shops for tourists and cafés selling food, and up flights of stairs were the cheap hotel rooms above. Further up was the famous Bazaar. Sultanahmet gave you, at some points, a view over the harbour and into the modern city and to the Asian part of Turkey.

The main streets of Sultanahmed were crowded with cars, vans, lorries and buses, none of them new. With horns tooting or blaring throughout the day, the Turkish drivers gesticulated and shouted. When they got up speed they were murderous. Turks would try to overtake anything slower than they were, and while there appeared to be pedestrian crossings marked on the roads there was no intention by any driver to stop at one. I saw one Turk in long robes bounced off the bonnet of a car, that slowed but didn't stop, as he tried to cross the road by the Bazaar.

The pavements also saw the bustle of Turks, the old men in traditional robes, the young and middle-aged Turkish men that dominated the sidewalks and the shops were in western clothes of T-shirts and trousers or jeans that were often ill-fitting. These men had short haircuts and moustaches and often one or more days growth of stubble that gave them a swarthy and unkempt appearance.

The Pudding Shop at the lower end of Sultanahmet spilled its crowded tables out onto the pavement and was the accepted gathering place for all westerners. Here a noticeboard was filled with a colourful and eclectic mix of cards and scraps of paper that gave advice to travellers, requests for lifts or messages for friends passing through. Here, in the place that some might think of as the start of the hippie trail itself, were accents and languages from all over the western world and English was the lingua franca.

Long haired, bearded white men in jeans and cheesecloth shirts, strolled casually with their pretty young women, all sandals, sunglasses, cotton dresses and shorts. Some girls were probably showing too much flesh in the sun, for the young Turkish women, even when in modern, colourful clothes, still covered their legs with slacks and often arms and heads too.

Sultanahmet was therefore rather like a European colony with scores of young Europeans, and North Americans too, exploring the shops, snack bars, the busy bazaar and going into and out of the cheap and very cheap hotels that provided little more than a bed and thin mattress to lie on.

In this white community of young travellers not everyone would be a signed-up hippie as previously described, although nearly all travellers would want to try to smoke some hashish on the way. Yes, there were the girls in flowered cotton dresses or shorts and sandals and the men in that uniform of western youth of faded bell-bottom jeans and cheesecloth shirts and beards and bangles. But not all would want the hard drugs or the eastern mysticism.

Pete was a quiet and thoughtful twenty something with a London East End accent. With skin the colour of tea stain, he probably had forebears who had been the foreign mix of any dockland area of sailors who had made that part of London their home or refugees escaping persecution in foreign lands. He was as English as I was. Pete wasn't short of money and had no embarrassment to tell you where his travel money had come from. Bumming around Europe for a couple of summers he had worked as a courier for coach holidays to Spain and later to Italy.

It was while in Rome that he had fallen out of the job and into the street, and life was tough on the streets of Rome. Sleeping under a bridge one night with local homeless youths they taught him how to rob the tourists for a living. He would engage UK or US tourists in conversation while the local lads did the pickpocketing.

'We would always watch and see where the tourists kept their money.' Pete explained. 'People will always tap the pocket their money is kept in; for reassurance,' he added. 'Then we made sure the tourist was on their own. I would start the conversation; two of them would start a fight so close to this man that they'd bump into us. Distracted he wouldn't see another youth behind steal his wallet or bag.' Pete said he had more sense than to try it out on the trail.

Second hand and battered transport, some showing flower decoration, lined up in the street. Coaches that were close to retirement, old ambulances with still some working life, an indestructible British double-decker bus, VW campers and dormobiles, all with number plates from most of the western European countries but mainly the UK, crowded the streets opposite the hotels and cafés. I noticed the Post Office logo on a couple of their former vans now appeared as an embossed print underneath some hastily sprayed new paint. Former ambulances had their own unique look and seemed totally out of place. They made great camper vans and rest places during the day as inhabitants planned journeys to India or back to the UK. Most owners only slept in their transport if they were desperate and seemed to mostly use the hotels.

While many hippies and westerners were travelling to India by this motley collection of own transport, including coaches like Budget Bus that were going all the way with its own load of paying passengers, others of us planned to use the local trains and buses, as Harold had suggested.

Hippie or tourist? I was asked. Neither. Some of us were just travellers and adventurers. We wanted to look, see, touch and to feel inwardly an experience of cultural escape. To travel as far as our money would take us. Besides, with no tourist book guides of the kind that we would find today in most bookshops to describe the history and culture of the countries we passed through, we didn't really know what there was to see, until we got there.

No-one I met sported a camera. Not even me. Today the 'selfie' would be happening all the time with the Blue Mosque and the varied historic and religious buildings of

Sultan Ahmed as the backdrop. For the tens of thousands who did the trip, few photos seem to record the events. I could not afford a camera, not even a Kodak Instamatic, but there was probably not anywhere to get the film developed after Istanbul or before Delhi. No one stayed long enough in any town or city on the trail in those days before instant developing, except perhaps in Kabul.

Back then, the experiences hippies and many travellers sought could be bought in small packets in back streets or hotel entrances from young Turks with quick movements, darting eyes and soft voices and be enjoyed in private and held on the inward eye until memory faded. You didn't need a camera for that; to do what you could not do legally in your own western European country.

'Yeah, some of us just want the hash, man,' said a dewy-eyed room companion to me as he lay on his bed, heavy-lidded staring up at the peeling ceiling.

Whether they have described themselves as hippies, travellers or tourists, I think most would still come to marvel at the sights of other cultures and countries on their travels. There was the Top Kapi Museum and the Blue Mosque here in Istanbul; the giant Buddhas carved into rock in the Bamiyan valley in Afghanistan; the Hindu Golden Temple in Amritsar or even the Himalayas at Katmandu. But nobody was too sure what there might be to see in Iran.

Others maybe were wanting something of the Beatles experience of eastern religions and ultimately to pray, chant or simply to meditate. For while Hinduism and Buddhism and other religions from the Indian sub-continent were of interest to the hippie culture, Islam with its rigid social rules and cultural practices held little interest for most. So, while the Mosques of Istanbul were visited because they were close to the hotels and the Pudding Shop, the other religious sites of Islam, including the beautiful mosques in Isfahan and elsewhere were often bypassed.

The propagation of a shame society where pride, honour, public conduct and appearance count for everything was not for hippies. They were people who wanted to make their own thoughts and conduct themselves without social constraints. Life was to be explored – not to feel guilty about.

The hippie lifestyle was the antithesis of Muslim culture and within a few short years the Muslim countries on this Old Silk Road would have rejected western values for Islamic fundamentalism of different kinds.

The hotels in Sultanahmed sounded exotically enticing and were, I recall, ridiculously named like Peace, Exotic or Beautiful. Like the Magic Bus, much imagination was needed for they were small, bare rooms sparsely furnished with narrow wooden beds. The Turkish exchange rate at that time was 30 Lirasi to the English pound (GB£) and to spend a night in one of these hotels was between 10 and 15 Lirasi, depending if you shared a room and how many beds were in the room.

With two others from the Magic Bus, I spent the first couple of days investigating the area. We walked up to the huge, covered bazaar with its trinket shops with long-robed

sellers standing proudly and expectantly in front of their wares hoping to entice you in to see their goods of metal-work, leather, jewelry, embroidery, wood carvings and all manner of foods, spices, fabrics and clothing. Keeping your money, Travellers cheques and passport, secure was the main and first priority for all of us. The only way was to keep them close to the body at all times, either in a body belt or a leather pouch to be hung around your neck. So, for most of us the belt or pouch was the first thing you would need to buy on your first morning. And this would probably be the first time you had ever needed to haggle to buy.

In the crowded bazaar, the gowned owner of a leath-erwork stall would greet you knowing exactly what you were looking for, for he had seen too many of your type before and had watched you eyeing up his goods before you had even glimpsed him. The price was always ridiculously high, for an Istanbul Turk enjoyed the game and the chal-lenge and the relationship formed in the haggling process. Cultural embarrassment was the problem to us young Brits, whose parents would never complain about poor service or shoddy goods. No one I met could take the negotiation down very far for anything, but the boast was that they did.

Walking back frustrated and emptyhanded from the bazaar, having surveyed the goods and prices and seen at-tempts at haggling and knowing I was not up to the public humiliation that a bazaar purchase might bring me, I saw what I wanted in the window of a shop. Entering in and pointing to the item in the window, I was asked a ridiculous price for a leather pouch. I made an offer below the price and with no negotiating skills I knew I had paid much more than I needed.

The sounds you woke to in your bare budget room in the early morning were of the imams calling the faithful to prayer over loudspeakers from the minarets of the Blue Mosque; the minarets of other mosques too competed for daily prayers. You didn't get the impression that mosques were well attended in the cities. Life for the modern Turk, at that time, seemed no longer directed too much by imams, but by their economic needs like most of Europe's peoples.

While impressive within its buildings, outside of the Blue Mosque not only was Sultanahmet a somewhat neglected and shabby part of Istanbul, but beyond the perimeter of the Mosque's compound was an area of neglected rough ground with shrubs and trees adjacent to the west wall. Not even what could be called a garden.

I didn't stay long in Istanbul. Sharing the room at the Hotel Beautiful was a young man who spoke very little English and knew he had very little hope of getting across Turkey to India without someone to help him along. Arald was tall, quiet and Norwegian. I wasn't sure if the quietness was simply his lack of English and there was no great con-

YAPI ve KREDİ BANKASI A. Ş.

1422   E   N̈ 81823

Tarih / Date :	13.6.1976

Döviz satanın adı ve Soyadı / Bought from :

Satın alınan dövizin cinsi - miktarı / Foreign Currency	Uygulanan kur / Rate	Ödenen Türk parası tutarı / Turkish Lira
£ 6.— ÇEK	32.30	193.80
		193.80

YAPI ve KREDİ BANKASI A. Ş.
Şubesi / branch

H/A

1/3

versation outside of the basic necessities of the day. My brother later spent some time in Norway in the 80s and said they all spoke perfect English.

'Why?' I asked.

'Well, why would anybody learn a language only five million people speak. So, Norwegians have to learn other people's languages.'

'By the way,' he added, 'if you ever forget my address, just put my name on the letter and NORWAY, and as the post-boat travels up the fiords, someone will know someone who knows someone who will have heard of me. It may take some weeks, but it will still get to me. Norway is a big village really.'

With a bit of Arald's schoolboy English and some sign language we decided we would take the train to Erzerum, the capital of Eastern Turkey. An express train would take us direct to Tehran in Iran, the next country, for 250TL. It would take 3 or 4 days, but it only left on Wednesdays, and it was now Wednesday, and the train had already departed.

We chose the cheaper option anyway and took the two-day train ride to Erzerum that would allow us to see something of the country and its people and how they lived.

Chapter 4

Erzerum

Thursday 13th June, and Arald and I took the ferry and crossed the busy waterway from Old Istanbul and the European mainland to Hyderpasha Station on the Asian side of Turkey from where the train to Erzerum would leave. Walking up a side street from the ferry terminal we came across a group of smartly uniformed soldiers carrying a coffin, rotating in turns to hold the weight of their dead colleague, seeing it as a privilege to do so but making an uncomfortable ride for the deceased.

The train ticket cost us 61TL each, which was around £2.00 for a seat on the train. Another 25L would have given us a sleeping berth, but neither of us wanted to afford it so we hoped the seat would be enough. We left Istanbul that evening at 10pm and expected to arrive in Erzurum on Saturday afternoon. After all, we were travelling from probably the western-most Turkish city to that furthest east.

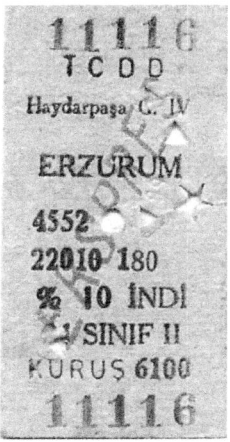

It was to be a good 42-hour train ride and we bought food of fruit, cheese and bread in the market stalls for the journey. By contrast an intercity train ride from London would, in five or six hours, take you to nearly all the major cities of England and another couple of hours to most of those in Scotland as well.

The journey started off well, for we managed to get a compartment on the train to ourselves. However, sleep for Arald and I was almost impossible with the rolling and rumbling of the train and the frequent stops. For at each successive stop through the first night more people joined the train, so that by about 3am our compartment was completely full and the corridor too. A group of young, happy, engaging Turkish youths who knew how to travel in comfort, burst in and swung themselves up onto the overhead luggage racks while the rest of us slept on the floor or hunched up on the seats.

The heat of the night and the smell of their unwashed bodies and clothes was almost overpowering. By morning these young, courteous and smiling Turks insisted on trying out some words of English they knew. A conversation that depended on signs as much as words. Fun as this was, I made a mental note that if I was to make the return journey on this train I would make sure I had the extra 25 Lirasi for the sleeper.

At some point nature called and making my way down the crowded corridors I found the toilet at the end of a carriage. I pushed open the door and stumbled in and, with the carriage swaying, slammed the door. My first shock was that it was dark. It took a few moments to get my bearings. I was in an empty windowless room with a flickering light from somewhere on the floor like a projector running a film.

As my eyes got used to the darkness, I could make out a round hole in the floor from where the light was coming.

The flickering was the rhythm of the railway sleepers sliding past the hole; black sleeper - grey stones - black sleeper - grey stones. Beside the hole on each side was the raised pattern of a large shoe and from the pattern one could see that they were to be used for squatting. The floor was wet, everywhere. I decided there would be no squatting for me on this train and did my small business towards the hole as best I could.

About 10am on Friday morning we arrived in Ankara, and two of our young Turks departed and two young European women got into our compartment. They told us we were chosen as we were the only Europeans that they could see on the train. Jacqueline was French and had been working in Israel on a kibbutz and was now trying to get to India and work there. Sophie was Swedish and was heading for the hippie trail too. Now Jacqueline, Sophie, Arald and I and the young Turks who were still with us, shared the food we each had including tomatoes, cucumbers and a very dry flat bread the Turks had brought for their journey.

The presence of blond, blue-eyed Sophie and the dark and bright-eyed Jacqueline was of great amusement to the young Turks, unused to close proximity to women not of their own family group, or particularly of independent western women travelling alone. They watched with amusement the noisy banter of instant friendships of four strangers in foreign lands.

The journey the length of Turkey had been slow and ponderous, and while it was called the Erzurum Express there was nothing express about it. At its fastest the train might have reached 30 - 40 miles an hour, with very many stops at small and large towns and some villages. The train became intensely crowded, with people standing throughout the narrow corridors. Arald and I did, with considerable effort, manage to squeeze, edge and beg our way down the train past countless Turks and over their bags and boxes, to find the restaurant car and have a cup of tea.

Turkish men were in western clothes, the women often in colourful full-length robes with scarves thrown over their heads. Many seemed to be heading to the market in the next town or city or returning from a market, judging by their possessions. None were tourists.

Determining that a return journey along the over-crowded corridors would be ill advised, we waited until the train stopped at another rural station. Most were without platforms and so we climbed down and walked along beside the track while people were unloading themselves, battered suitcases, kids and bags and baskets of all sizes. Others were getting onboard with their families, goods and chattels. As we came to our carriage we climbed aboard.

On one occasion, after a visit to the restaurant car, the wheels groaned and squealed and began to grip as Arald and I ran along beside the track. As the train began to move, we leapt onto the steps of our carriage to the amusement of the Turks standing in the crowded doorway who heaved us aboard.

The dry barren landscape of Turkey was quite breath-taking at times contrasting with snow-capped mountain peaks we could see in the distance and river gorges to pass through. But we had little sleep during the second night either, with the heat of the day throughout the train almost up to 90°F, and the aroma of our kind and friendly young Turks.

We Europeans were a curiosity in rural Turkey; mustachioed men of all ages seemed to have travelled from far parts of the train and would stand at the door of our compartment and simply stare at the four of us. Yes, they just stared. None of them were at all socially embarrassed to be doing this. A few would then try out some words of English that they knew. One little boy of about five, who at the door shouted out, 'One two three five four', felt very proud of himself for our approval of his language skills.

We arrived at Erzurum station about 4pm on Saturday. Exhausted from sleepless nights, we staggered off the train with our backpacks and headed up the platform for the exit. It was as hot as Istanbul but not nearly so humid.

Erzerum: I had imagined a modern city, for it was a regional capital after all. Outside the station a modern dual carriageway beckoned, and we could see buildings about a quarter of a mile away. But, hang on a minute, no motor cars on the road?

Two horse-drawn carriages with battered black canopies and each with a mangy horse were standing listless in the heat. The carriages looked like they dated from the Victorian era. Each had a bearded driver in turban, long gown and whip, who now looked up from their afternoon nap, indicating a taxi ride.

There were now six of us, for elsewhere on the train had been Harald and Lisbeth, also from the Magic Bus. He was Danish and she Swedish and they were at university together in Copenhagen. In spite of the heat, we all decided to save our money and walk. The horses snorted, grateful I think, for the continued rest.

The tarmacked dual carriageway led to buildings and a small shopping area. However, as soon as we arrived, the carriageway disappeared and so did the main road. We looked around, confused. It looked like we were in a town square with a few concrete buildings, offices and shops to give some semblance of civic pride. Off the main area we could see the rest of the low buildings were a shanty town of small, ground floor dwellings.

It wasn't that the area was poor or that the buildings were poorly constructed. That was not the case. There were no street names, houses got in the way of paths and alleyways, little tarmac, no cohesiveness or organization to it. No town planner seemed to have ever visited this side of town. I never found out if this was the centre of Erzerum or a suburb.

A few 1950s chrome laden, American cars with cracked, white-walled tyres swayed slowly about these by-ways and lanes. Between them, horses and mules with sores from harnesses and whose flanks stretched over ribs that could be counted, pulled carts and carriages with buckled wheels and shabby canopies. Many of the animals were well past their working lives and would probably die in harness. In the mountains around us, and in spite of summer, snow still lay in sheltered areas close to the tops overlooking the city.

Hotel Hazor, 4 stories high, paraded itself above the houses and small shops in the centre of another square. Harald did the negotiating for us. Other small 'otels' or hotels had wanted 15TL a night, but Harald got the price down to 12TL each. We had spartan rooms at the top of the building, opening out onto the roof and in the freshening air we rested for about an hour. Then, as evening approached, we decided to explore the town for food, and the transport for the next part of our journey that would take us into Iran.

Together, the six of us toured the small shopping area. We ate at an open-air café, at a scattering of wooden tables and a variety of chairs, the only customers - and passers-by stopped and stared. This was something we were going to have to get used to from here on. None of the people meant us any harm.

Harald and Lisbeth had a hippie trail travel booklet and knew the next destination from here. We needed a coach that would take us through Dogubayazit (known on the trail as 'dodgy-biscuit') to the Iranian border.

Back in England, my friend Harold's advice about money had been, 'If you are travelling through countries without staying long, take small denomination Travellers cheques. That way you are not left with a pile of money you cannot use in the next country.' The next day I would find a bank and change just enough money to pay for the ticket on to Tehran.

As we finished the meal and began to look for a coach company's offices - they found us. As young Europeans in the street they knew what we wanted. Together, three young Turks, welcoming and voluble, began to vie for our travel needs. We again left it to Harald's persuasive and confident manner to negotiate for us. One company was pressing hard for our business.

'Nice comfy seat,' he claimed smiling beneath his black moustache, 'and cassette tape for music. Rock music. You like?'

I said wearily and cynically from the side-lines, 'Oh, and I expect you give free Coca Colas too.' To which he looked up at me with not a blink and said, 'Oh yes, we do. Air conditioning too.'

Our seats on his Mihan Tour coach would cost us 115TL each. We booked it!

The business done for the evening, the others moved on back to the hotel. Harald and I wanted to explore and walked away curious about the shanty town. Beyond the shopping area there were no formal streets, but nameless lanes and alleys and pathways. Quickly we found ourselves

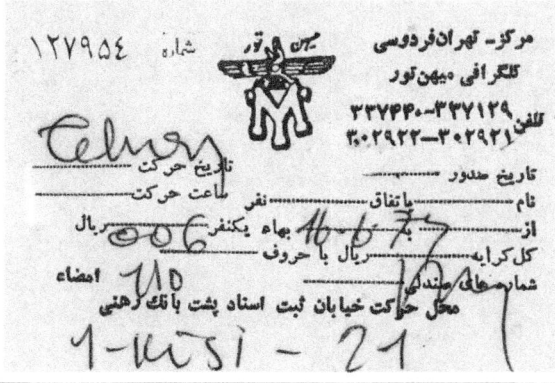

amongst the self-designed, single-story dwellings. Many were well-constructed, while others formed in bare brick or breezeblocks just lacked much of a plan in their construction. Children played in the streets, women watched us from alleyways and an occasional animal-drawn transport passed. Our curiosity somewhat satisfied we turned back for the hotel, and we stared blankly at the road we had just walked down, confused.

Without street names and the lack of any significant identifying factor in the low buildings, we had no clue of the path we had taken. Alleyways led off to the right. Had we come this way? We turned into one which we thought we recognised. But we were wrong. The random nature of the dwellings gave no clue to what we might have passed and there were no high-rise buildings to see or shops from which we could get our bearings. The narrowness of the dirt streets and pathways meant we could get no view of the four-storey Hotel Hazor.

We stopped passers-by – no one spoke English. A woman stood in a doorway; she shook her head to our questions.

A large, old American saloon car with imperfect

T. C. ZIRAAT BANKASI   TÜRK LİRASI
TEDİYE FİŞİ

Döviz satanın adı soyadı
ve adresi   № 072392
Satın alınan Dövizin :

CİNSİ	MİKTARI	UYGULANAN KUR	TUTARI TL.	H. S. No.	BORÇLU HESAPLAR
	2	32.70	65.60	403. EFEKTİF ALIM VE SATIMI	

ALACAKLI HESAP 001 (KASA)

YALNIZ   LİRA   KR.

YUKARIDA YAZILI EFEKTİFLER (İN) / TAHSİL EDİLMİŞTİR / TAHSİLİ MUKABİLİNDE / ÖDEYİNİZ.
PARAFLAR   İMZALAR

chrome was squeezing its way through the narrow streets and we waved him down. He put his head out of the window, but he understood not a word we spoke. We walked on for several minutes. We were getting desperate now as dusk was falling and there was no street lighting.

Suddenly a soldier in uniform appeared from the next bend and immediately Harald was animated.

'He will probably speak some German,' he said. 'The German army still trains the Turks. Germany has a long history with the Ottoman Empire and were allies in the First World War,' he explained.

Harald knew enough German for our needs for immediately the soldier's eyes lit up. A few words, gestured hands, questions and thanks, and within a few minutes we were back at the shopping area and the Hazor hotel. The shanty town of Erzerum was the one place where English was not the lingua franca on the trail!

At 6am the next morning, we gathered at Mihan Tour offices and there stood a modern coach that put the Magic Bus to shame. With comfy seats of plush red fabric, we travelled in some style listening to the Beatle's Sergeant Pepper album, a bit dated perhaps, but does pop or rock ever date? Or something heavier like Roxy Music or Status Quo. True to the promise, bottles of Coca Cola in ice buckets covered the back seat for us to refresh ourselves with on the journey.

To our joy, the air-conditioning too kept the summer temperature down. With music over the speakers, we headed for Agri and then on to Dogubayazit where I changed some money into Iranian Rials. Later, as we approached the border, we passed the snow-covered peaks of Greater and Lesser Ararat rising steeply above the expanse of endless plain.

Did Noah really beach his ark there?

Chapter 5
Iran

We crossed into Iran at the Bazargam border on the afternoon of Sunday 16th June. Visas for the US and European citizens were scrutinized by the smartly uniformed Iranian officials, while my British passport was just date stamped. Later in the day we passed through the city of Tabriz.

Travelling with us was Amir, who was heading home to Tehran for a family wedding. His cousin, Nouri, had finally agreed to marry at the age of thirty-five, at his family's insistence, having now set up his own motor business.

'Selling Iranian designed cars is not where the most profit is,' Amir smiled and insisted as he smoothed his moustache and offered me small tomatoes from his food bag. He then proudly told me that he himself usually spent his time driving brand new Mercedes cars from the factory in Germany to rich owners his brother would find in Iran.

'That is where the big profits are, my friend; Mercedes, BMW. The rich people want to show off their wealth.' He laughed. 'What is the point of money if you cannot show it off?'

He said, he would soon be travelling back to Germany for the next new car order and Mihan Tour would take him all the way to Munich from Tehran. The owner of three smart restaurants in the top end of the city had put the order in to the German factory for the latest Mercedes car which was now ready to travel. He was booked for the first of next month to travel to collect the vehicle.

'About seven or eight a year, I do. It's a good living and a lot of fun.'

Through a dry and desert landscape and with drinks on board, Mihan Tours was making the minimum of stops. But as evening drew on, we pulled over to where a roadside outdoor café produced for us a mouth-watering Tabriz speciality of beef with onions and walnuts, with slices of off-white bread and my first taste of chickpeas.

No new travellers joined us, and with the music and lights off, we slept through the darkest of nights with the brightest and clearest of starlight bouncing along above us until, early the next morning, Monday, we awoke to a cacophony of noise in the centre of Tehran.

It was about 7am. But none of us seemed to notice because the streets were an extraordinary jam of motionless, hooting vehicles, mainly of Iranian make, with intolerant drivers whose windows were down in the already 80-degree heat, shouting and gesticulating to anyone and everyone. Traffic disorder was at an altogether different level to Istanbul motorists. Here, there were so many vehicles that nothing moved, not even when the traffic lights changed. Such a contrast again to the shanty Erzurum with its dusty roads and mixture of battered cars and horse-drawn cabs.

Tehran boasted that it was a modern city under the Shah, modelling itself on western values of business, i.e., avarice and commercialism, rather than its historic Muslim identity. It showed, and I could understand the advice from travellers in the Pudding Shop not to stay long in Tehran.

The Shah kept secret police to harass his enemies and possession of drugs was illegal. The advice in Harald's guide was to stay as short a time in Iran as possible – there was no fun for a hippie or adventurer to be had here – just drive straight on to Mashad and then the border with Afghanistan. That was where the fun and real adventure was to be found.

The Central Post Office was opposite our stop. We crossed the wide street safely in the motionless traffic and went to see if any mail had arrived for us. Before the invention of the mobile phone, families could write to you ahead of your arrival at a town. This essential stop at the 'Post-Restante' desk of a post office anywhere in the world was the place to catch up with news from family and friends. Before I set out I had calculated my travel times with suggestions to family members of where and when they could write to me.

The young official took my surname and picked from the enlarged pigeonhole a clump of letters and we thumbed through them together. There were no letters for me. Disappointed, I knew I had been travelling very quickly and perhaps too quickly for mail from England to catch up with me just yet. Others were luckier.

Out again in the sun, the six of us quickly decided that we needed somewhere to wash off the dust and sweat of travel. I thought the main railway station might have some facilities. Harald, dependable as always, found a bus to take us there for we didn't want to walk far in this heat.

But we were to be disappointed, for on arrival we found it was a relatively small, drab station building with nothing to meet our needs. The station in this capital city was not the bustling transport hub of a station in most European cities.

The modernisation of Tehran's new values, that seemed to be a loosening of Muslim social constraints, was symbolised for me by a large building carrying a huge sign for a very western fast-food outlet – WIMPY. It oversaw a roundabout of parched grass and flowerbeds containing a large statue of the Shah.

The heat was dry and becoming intense under the pale blue sky that became paler each hour as more dust was thrown into the air by human activity. There were no large stores and the streets of small shops, cafés and drink stalls with open fronts were individually owned, each selling almost the same things as his neighbour.

In every shop, very visible for all to see, were large, framed photos of the Shah, sometimes with his wife. This was not necessarily a symptom of the affection felt for the monarch, like shopkeepers in Victorian England might have felt for Queen Victoria. The secret police needed to know where your loyalties lay.

Traders were everywhere and different roads and sections of the city's commercial area seemed to have particular trades they specialised in; engineering and motor repairs, household fabrics and furnishings, fresh food and spices, etc. Some of the smaller shops on the streets, shuttered when closed and with homemade signs, sold snacks and drinks; Coca Cola and 7Up of course. But the local speciality, and on your choice of fruits or vegetables, enough would be quickly peeled and sliced and put into the blender and within a minute the smoothie drink was yours. It was to be years before this caught on in Britain.

Pedestrian crossing markings gave a semblance of civility on the road, but when the traffic moved drivers ignored them, and the noise of hooting and shouting was continuous in the now slow-moving traffic. Traffic lights were mere street ornaments with cars heading in the same direction sometimes on both sides of the road. Many cars wore some kind of injury beneath their film of dust.

The dress of all Iranian men was western. Most older women wore long dresses or robes that covered the arms with some sort of head covering from a scarf to a hijab, depending on their state of liberalisation. Younger women I saw could wear slacks and tee-shirts, and most often with a head covering. Others wore darkly patterned robes, and while they walked with eyes often cast down to show modesty, their head covering was often nominal, and they would let their flower-patterned, silk head-veils slip in the breeze to the back of their head or shoulder as they laughed with their girlfriends. I didn't get the impression that Iranian women needed a man in order to walk freely in the street.

The temperature was now about 85°F and so with the heat, the traffic, the fumes and the knowledge that most of my coach companions were heading for Afghanistan for simply one purpose, meant that the six of us all decided we didn't want to stay in Tehran or Iran any longer than necessary.

Back at the coach, Mihan Tour would be very happy to take us to the next city on the hippy trail, Meshad, that afternoon. Tehran to Meshad was a fifteen-hour journey by coach
for 350Rials and we heard that from there we could get a bus to Taybad on the border with Afghanistan which would cost another 100Rials and take about 4 hours.

We left at 2pm, and the music machine soon sucked a tape into its innards. We travelled with no music to kill the time, but the air conditioning was refreshing and the free and cool Coca Colas still flowed.

Iran is a huge country that seemed thinly populated across its dry barren wastelands. As the evening drew on we began a long climb up into the mountains. Looking to the north we could see into the former USSR, Russia, and the vastness of the Caspian Sea slate-blue and motionless stretching away to the horizon. We slept huddled in the seats because the night was cold. We stopped a couple of times and whispered voices from the front of the bus woke those who needed a toilet or food break.

Outside the coach, the Milky Way was again sparkling bright in the heavens against the jet-black screen of eternity. Why can it never be that way in England? I thought, remembering how the yellow, sodium street lighting in Bristol in those times concealed the night sky and then confused the colours in the street.

The wayside open-air eating place was lit only by glowing braziers covered in wide pans of food and a dim lamp powered from the small one story building behind. Shadowy figures in robes stood by as I examined the pans wondering what was on offer. Through a process of elimination, we settled on rice, meat and potatoes, but what the meat was this time we had no idea.

Tall, western Europeans like me found the seats in the coach too cramped for much sleeping. The light in the sky woke me early that Tuesday morning although the sun was still hidden behind the mountains. Two hours later we reached Mashad just as the shops were having their shutters taken down and opening for trade.

'Hey, guys, let's sell blood here in Mashad,' said Harald.

'Seven dollars a pint,' chipped in Lisbeth. 'We could all use the money, yes?' she said, pulling a wisp of wavy blond hair behind her ear.

'Oh, yes we could!' we chorused.

The sale of blood to hospitals in the Arab countries was a popular way of getting some extra cash on the trail, so said the underground travel leaflets. As there was nothing to see or attract us to the town of concrete shops, motor cars and rising temperatures, Harald, Lisbeth, Arald and I hailed a cruising saloon taxi and asked the driver to take us to the Red Cross hospital. Seven US dollars may not sound a lot now, but it was much more then, and in Asia the money could get you through a few days.

'You can sell it in Greece too on the way home if you need to.' Harald was well into getting the most from this trip.

The Red Cross hospital had no idea about buying blood from anyone. The white uniformed woman at the reception desk shook her head, not understanding too much English and looked surprised as we indicated veins in arms. We returned to the taxi, looked back at the building and realised that this was not *The* Red Cross hospital but simply a hospital with a red cross.

We needed our taxi driver now to know exactly what we wanted if we were going to succeed with this venture. He scratched his black moustache and rubbed his 3-days growth. Then a light burst into his eye with a smile. We bundled back into his machine full of hope again.

Five minutes later we were outside another drab, grey, building that had the universal red sign of a medical facility but with Arabic writing above. Clearly a hospital, but was it *the* Red Cross hospital?

In the reception area someone spoke some English. Great! No, they didn't buy blood. They knew of nowhere that would buy blood. They frowned and thought it seemed a strange thing to ask. Then we tried to emphasise that it was the Red Cross hospital that we wanted. Was that them? They shook their heads.

We tried once more with the taxi driver, trying to hide our disappointment, giving him all the encouragement to get us what we were after. He was disappointed too and knit his brows, puzzled as to exactly where he had gone wrong. Okay, he would try again.

Another drive around largely deserted roads of featureless buildings. This time he did get us to *The* Red Cross Hospital with much cheering and thanks. But the door was locked. There was no explanation and access to it seemed impossible. No-one could be found. Much disappointment from us all as $7 would have been most useful. We had no more time to waste on this. We thanked our driver; he was sorry. We told him it was OK. Now he could help us with just one more thing.

At another grey, concrete structure we followed the signs and climbed the stairs to knock on the door of the Afghan Consulate. Our visas cost 350 Rials (165 Rials to the GB£) and had our passports stamped with their official seal.

Others thought the charge for the visa was a '*ripoff*', meaning that they thought we should have got this for free or not paid so much.

Ripoff was a hippie word I really heard for the first time on this trip. Another word new to me was '*hassle*' meaning to have an argument over money or with authorities. I couldn't complain. Most continentals and those from North America had been paying for visas in every country we had passed through. Not so the British. In my long journey through Europe and across Asia this was the only visa I was required to purchase. Pax Britannica made this possible.

The robed official pointed to signs on the walls and the door of the Embassy warning us that the new regime in Afghanistan, recently installed, had ruled that long hair on men was not acceptable in their country and it would be cut at the border if required; and drug use in public areas was also banned. I had neither long hair nor an interest in drugs.

A few doors down we found a bank and exchanged pounds and dollars for Afghanis; 140Afgns to the GB£.

We left Mashad for Taybad and the border in the afternoon for 100 Rials each, and, travelling up into the mountains, arrived on a dusty road on a high plateau at the modern but very remote border buildings just before 7pm and went through the Iranian formalities quickly. We were the only travellers at that hour.

Border guards in peaked caps and American style uniforms told us that the border into Afghanistan closed at 7.30pm and that there was a mile or more of no-man's-land between us and Afghanistan. We couldn't see their border post and the road from here on was unpaved; the sun had set and a chill was in the evening air. Already some of us could feel that this was more than a physical border to cross. None of us fancied the walk. Was there any transport?

The Mihan Tour coach had returned to Mashad after dropping off its load of western youth. Now on exiting the building we saw another coach looking dusty and disheveled parked at the side of the road. Questions were asked and we were told this was the transport that travelled through no-man's-land to Afghanistan. There were some raised voices and pleadings to the officials from our companions and finally a driver was found to drive us the short mile before the border closed.

Old and dirty and nobody's first choice for transport it may have been, but we clambered aboard as its driver grumbled the beast into life, grinding it into gear to the cheers of those who saw this as being the last mile to their country of destination.

None of us sat down. We all stood in the gangway willing the bus to reach the other side before nightfall set in and the border closed. It might have been quicker to walk, but finally the reluctant vehicle swung off the roadway into an encampment of single-story mud brick buildings that had no signs of any kind.

Unsmiling turbaned officials greeted us in traditional Afghan dress of dark green, baggy trousers, black army boots, long collarless green shirts to the knees, sleeveless dark waist coats, bandoliers of bullets and full untrimmed beards. The turban was not a neatly folded, dinghy style, Sikh turban close fitting to provide mutual recognition. These had enough cloth to clothe a small child but were coiled atop a scraggy bearded and black-eyed head in the manner of clothes thrown into a laundry basket.

One had a white turban and a white shirt with a grey waistcoat who seemed to take charge. He didn't have a bandolier of bullets across his chest and while his shirt like all the others was collarless, I guessed the white meant he was the white-collar worker. His chest was larger than his compatriots and his voice louder. But as we heaved our bags off the coach we had a shock in store.

'Border closed.' The official in white scowled and re-peated himself and pointed to his watch. The hands indicated it was already 8.30pm; not 7.30pm.

'No bus tonight. Stay here. You sleep here.' This was not a conversation or a question. It was a statement of fact. Someone offered the man a passport. He refused it. 'To-morrow, tomorrow,' he snapped. We were confused until one of us realised we must have passed a time-zone in that dusty mile from Iran.

Chapter 6
Afghan Border to Kandahar

Not unfriendly, but not a welcome smile either. They were just doing their job. Probably in their eyes we were all infidels and destined for hell anyway. Maybe they understood that most of us were not here to admire their grand mosques for they had none to rival either Turkey or Iran's Muslim magnificence. They had their own idea of why we were here, and they would not distinguish between the hippies who had come for only one purpose, and those of us tourists or travellers also dressed in jeans and tee-shirts for whom their cities or village life, deserts or their lush valleys, remote mountains and wildlife might draw some interest.

The hippies purpose grew in their valleys. Hashish and

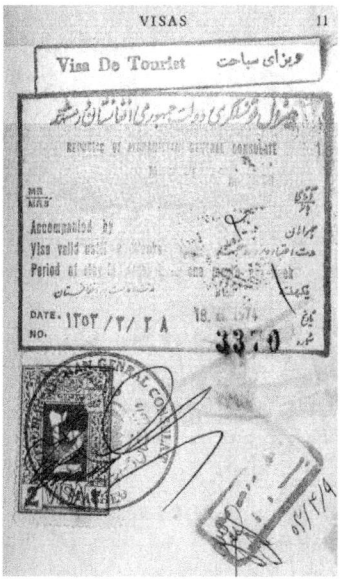

opium were harvested by poor farmers to be sold on, and much to be smuggled by others out of the country to foreign states in the western world, who shared neither their religion, values nor their culture. If the freedom-loving hippies were subverting the strict laws of Afghan society and culture from their travels into the country, a kind of subtle undoing of western values in Europe was at work in Afghanistan's most famous exports.

Afghanistan was a place in transition. The traditional king Zahir Shah who had had the loyalty of the disparate tribes in a huge country, had been deposed in a bloodless coup the previous year by the king's cousin Daoud Khan. The country had become a republic and there was talk of women's rights and modernization. Yet now even that first Revolutionary Council of Daoud's had also been replaced, without bloodshed, with one supported this time by the communist Soviet Union.

This new Second Revolutionary Council was keen to tighten up on its international reputation as the world's leading recreational drug producer, by cutting back on the production of the drugs in the rural districts and banning the use and sale of drugs in public areas. To discourage hippies and appease the tribal Muslim leaders they threatened to have the long hair cut off men at the border.

In the collection of flat-topped one-story buildings of mud brick that made up the scattered border post there were no signs of any kind to indicate any organisation. Nevertheless, the presence of a couple more white-turbaned officials without bandoliers of bullets gave the place a kind of officialdom.

We asked for a hotel. 'Yes. Come.'

We followed.

In the gathering gloom we were shown into a windowless hut of earthen floor and two rooms. The turbaned officials gathered in the centre of the room, and one reached up and turned on the one, bare electric light. Suddenly, 10,000 doodoos erupted from the walls and surrounded it in flight. Some were as large as small birds casting flickering shadows onto the earthen walls. We stood back and kept our heads down and mouths shut.

A white-shirted official told us we could stay here on the bare floor for 20Afgs each per night and promised us a meal. There seemed no choice as the sun was now well gone and twilight disappearing. They served us bowls of the inevitable meat and gravy with the dry, corrugated bread that we ripped up and used to scoop up and eat as we sat on the dusty earth outside.

It was only after we had eaten the meal and paid up for it that two long-haired Brits came running up to say that they had found a superior place to stay nearby.

'Hey man, it's a proper guest house - with beds,' they enthused.

We thanked the disappointed officials, and then hiked our rucksacks over to more low buildings in the far corner of the site.

The hotelier greeted us with a smile of absent teeth and, showing us the rooms, announced 20Afgs each for the night. The same price we had been offered for the bare earth with the doodoos. I shared a room with 4 others on wooden framed and slatted beds. The night was cold, and the sleeping bags now began to be useful, high up as we were, on Afghanistan's plateau.

The day begins early on the high plateau. A quick breakfast of the now familiar corrugated flat bread, this time with goats cheese, and we returned to the border huts of the night before. Here we went through the customs procedures. Passports and visas examined; bags searched. What for? I wondered.

'Man, they are looking for valuables; any kind of valuable item that might be sold at high value within their country and the money then taken and spent abroad. They write it in your passport, and you need to have it on you when you leave the country. Or big trouble.' One of us clearly had knowledge of how international trade and finance worked.

Finally, we also had to sign forms to declare exactly how much money we were bringing into the country. At one level I think they wanted to make sure we had 100 US dollars or equivalent in cash or Travellers cheques, in the expectation that we would be spending it all here.

Two guys with London accents clothed in crotch-tight jeans and rock tee-shirts and with immaculately groomed hair to their waists and short beards were told by a scowling baggy-trousered official with a huge, bushy, black beard, 'You must cut hair. No long hair!' This was going to be a test of the new rules.

'Man, I've spent five years growing this.' The guy smoothed his glossy hair down over his black Led Zep tee-shirt. 'It ain't comin' off for you guys.' He and his friend scoffed and turned away, laughing.

'Yeah, we'll go back down through southern Iran and through the border into Pakistan,' said Led Zep guy, looking in a mirror held up by an Afghan soldier. 'We kin wait to smoke hash in Kabul.' They caught the bus back to Mashad the next day.

Warnings were again given about the use of drugs in public places. The Second Revolutionary Council was determined to improve the reputation of their country regarding the drug trade, and so after our bags were searched, scissors were found for the hippies who were prepared to lose their hair and snip it to an agreed length; some did. The prize of Kabul was only a few days travel through Herat and Kandahar. Some had spent years growing and nurturing long hair and so the sacrifice was greater and for some too much. Confusingly, there was no restriction on the length of beards which to Afghan males was a source of pride.

The contrast with westernised Iran was considerable. Somehow we were impressed that the Afghan officials had kept to the same traditional Afghan dress they had worn for centuries and had not given way to the Iranian ideas of western culture and clothing. This country was much poorer, yet there seemed to be some kind of integrity here, an authenticity in the people, that would not give way to the simple commercialism across the border and further west. This had some positive comparisons with hippie values, it seemed. At this point none of us had seen their women, confined and hidden under burqas, whose every move was controlled by their men.

The formalities over, eight of us squeezed into a pale blue VW minibus labelled the 'Afghan Post Bus Company' waiting to take us into Herat for 50Afgs, about a three-hour ride away. The earth was barren and, except where a stream or river ran at the side of the road and nurtured some green vegetation, this was desert with huge rocky outcrops on either side rising suddenly, as if erupting from the dry, barren earth.

We arrived in Herat just after 2pm and were dropped off at a hotel whose reputation in hippie literature was a 'flea-ridden dive'. But at this point we were so tired from our constant travelling that we all decided to stay at least one night here and catch up on lost sleep. It was now 12 days since I had left England and had been constantly travelling and dealing with the demands of each new country, new town, new transport, new cuisine, foreign peoples, travelling companions and officials at every moment, and it seemed as if I had been on the go for months.

At the Nawai Behzad hotel, a night in a shared room, with the risk of bed bugs departing residents told us, was 25Afgs. I risked it and shared a room with Arald, and Steve who had already been there a couple of days. Weary heads rested in the formless concrete building that provided some protection from the heat of the day. Dark staircases and bare walls and a wooden form 18inches off the ground with the thinnest of mattresses and a blanket provided some comfort.

Later I looked out of the shuttered rectangle at the street below. It was largely empty with an occasional colourless car or ancient long-nosed lorry with its engine cowlings long gone, and when they passed they were just functional and unrecognisable of any make. Here, unlike Tehran or Istanbul, there was no rush hour. An occasional noisy, dull and shabby box of a bus lumbered past and bony nags and enslaved donkeys dragged ageless carts and carriages of items of all kinds on buckled wooden wheels, or the discarded tyres from cars or lorries as their turbaned owners, carrying a long stick with a leather whip at the end, encouraged the animal and scraped a living.

Up to this point I had been travelling with the same group of companions. Arald, Harald and Lisbeth had been good company too, as well as the two girls who had joined us in Ankara. The following day, with Harald and Lisbeth, we got out the maps and talked about how to get to Kabul.

The options were simple. There was the desert road to Kandahar and then on to Kabul. That would be two days across the desert and the quickest. There was a four-day route across the mountains, and it would be cold and probably dangerous on the mountain roads. None of us had the money to fly if that was even an option. I decided to travel on to Kabul via Kandahar and hoped that summer in Kabul would be nicely cooler. Arald would stay a few more days and so would Harald and Lisbeth. But time for me was short. I needed to be back in England by the beginning of the academic year in September.

That afternoon, scrambling through the dusty and formless back streets on clear instructions from the hotelier,

I found the office of a bus company, largely recognizable
from the vehicles outside. Single-decker box-like local buses that I had seen earlier were standing by looking shabby
and exhausted, baking in the sun. As I bought a ticket to
Kabul for 90Afgs, I wondered where the coaches were, like
Mihan Tour, that travelled between the large cities; still
travelling I guessed.

Thursday evening, Steve came in stoned, swaying and
sleepy, as he had found a small hotel that had sold him hash
to smoke on their premises. After an hour or so he began to
recover, at which point Arald returned and together they lit
a reefer and smoked it. They offered it to me, but I was
bright-eyed, feasting on a large bunch of the sweetest
grapes I had bought at a stall for the equivalent of 4p and
washed in chlorinated water.

The temperature was up in the 90s during the day and

falling asleep under a single sheet as the nights turned colder I somehow contracted a summer cold. I was not feeling particularly well in my head when I woke, but it was 6am and the promise was to be in Kandahar by 3pm, just nine hours away. I had with me my red rucksack, some fruit and a large flask of water as I arrived expectantly at the offices of the bus company.

Now, Mihan Tour had spoilt me. Iran and even Turkey had spoilt me. I asked for the coach to Kandahar. They pointed to the afore-mentioned dusty and ill-treated metal box of a bus now filling up with Afghan men.

'This bus to Kandahar,' said the bearded bus rep forcefully to my confused face and repeated question, and his turbaned staff nodded. There was to be no air-conditioned coach. The transport throughout this country was by post-bus. This snub-nosed jallopy was it; a metal box on wheels from which I could already feel the heat radiating and which I knew instinctively would soon, if it wasn't already, be an oven on wheels. The sun was already well above the horizon and the heat of the day beginning to be intense. Oh fool! Of course, this was not a modern state. There could be no modern coaches, no Coca-Cola, no air conditioning and little comfort.

The travellers were mainly Pashtun men in traditional Afghan tribal dress. They loaded their live chickens onto the roof along with boxes and large linen bags where a young boy, smiling and hanging onto a young goat sat perched on the substantial roof-rack with a clutch of men now already squatting there with their bags and ready to go.

I stepped into the doorless entrance and showed my ticket to the humourless driver, and then I was climbing over huge sacks of corn and vegetables that had taken four men to drag on-board and which filled the gangway from front to back. I was followed on by the only other European travelling, a Danish girl with mousy-blond hair whose name was Ena. A long dress was essential in these parts, but her bare arms held the curious stares of the Afghan men. She quickly signalled to sit next to me, on the unforgiving wooden bench.

Ena was not the only female on the bus. Two or three Afghan men had brought along wives or daughters; it was impossible to know which for they were completely hidden under full-length pale blue or black burqas or chadarees leaving only a crochet latticework around the eyes for them to see out. Every now and then one caught the glint of an eye behind the tightly woven fabric. Light from a very dark place. Young or old - it was impossible to know - and their menfolk kept staring eyes away from them.

As the bus struggled to start and the gears rolled un-easily into place, the thought came to me that this was maybe not the best decision I had made. My shirt was al-ready soaked with my sweat and as we moved off it was clear that the metal box was well beyond overloaded. All the springs and shock absorbers had bust years past. The gears grumbled loudly as we lurched and stumbled from the dusty unpaved side-street up onto the tarmac of the main road, largely empty of any other motor traffic.

We were soon out of the town, past the ring of fields of crops and small orchards that helped support this city so far from the rest of the country. A sign said, 'Kandahar 450 kilometers' and only then did it dawn on me, as the bus struggled to get into fourth gear and achieve 50 kph, that to do this journey it would need to travel at 50kph non-stop all the way to arrive by 3pm. Could there possibly be any hope of that? My head ached; my stomach was asking me questions.

On either side of the desert road to Kandahar were again these huge outcrops of rock, barren of any plant growth and seemingly un-weathered by countless ages without rain. It was as if huge, giant tipper trucks had simply unloaded onto the barren earth a mountain of rubble rising 200 or 300 feet high under an intense, unforgiving and cloudless sky. This was the plain of Dasht-i-Margo, the desert of death. It would be no exaggeration to say that the temperature outside was over 100°F and inside the bus 20-30° more.

Within a few miles of the journey, my sweat engaged with the dust of the desert, blown in through the open windows, to create a shirt of cardboard and I genuinely thought that if I took it off it would stand of its own accord on the seat. Keep the windows open and the motion of hot air would dry you out. Close them, and you would roast in the oven.

Nevertheless, this desert road to Kandahar was smoother than I could ever have hoped for, tarmac all the way. However, within the hour we were making stops at communities along the road for small groups of people to get on top or inside the bus with more sacks and small animals added. I was amazed that in such remote, small communities Afghans could survive on their animals and what grew in the fields. Whatever I may have thought of this mode of transport, the post bus was a lifeline to the country's large town markets for these villagers.

By 11am the water I had brought had been exhausted between Ena and myself. She had bought some peaches and other fruit, but this was soon finished and finding a way of dealing with our increasing thirst became more urgent all the time.

The village stops on this main road were all making our journey time so much longer and as the bus pulled in, we could see children sitting in the shade of a building, under a thin tree or raised piece of cardboard. They rose expectantly in the hope of selling us glass bottles of Coca Cola in buckets of ice or fruit laid out in front of them. These were the 'café' stops and the Coke and the bus were the only items from the 20th century that we perceived on this trip, apart from the guns and bullets. Welcome as these stops were, they were only going to prolong our agony of the journey.

Afghan men got down and refreshed themselves with water or chai. The displays of fruits lay open on the ground, and they bought what they needed and took them to feed to their children, and the women who ate them under their head coverings on the bus. Ena and I bought Cokes, uncertain about eating unwashed fruit. But, despite the ice in the bucket, the bottles quickly warmed as we drank them. Where were they getting such big blocks of ice from in this desert?

Around noon, the post bus pulled over to the side of the road in a remote spot. The Afghan men climbed down from the roof or clambered over the sacks and, finding their own space twenty paces or so from the bus, some would do their toilet using a small brass teapot with a tall spout that they carried every journey with them. Then they all laid out their small prayer mat and deciding on the direction of Mecca bowed, knelt and prayed. Friday was their holy day. We would avert our eyes, waiting impatiently for the journey to continue.

We hoped to be in Kandahar by 3pm. But long before then we were both completely dehydrated. Our thirst and discomfort were becoming obvious to the man behind us. He was, incongruously, dressed in the uniform of the Afghan Airforce, clearly an officer. Whatever we had thought of the bus, it was without doubt a bus for every Afghan. He kindly offered us tomatoes, cucumber and salt that were his food for the journey. Such sensible food! He insisted and the cucumber lived up to its appellation – cool; it was so cool to eat in this oven of a bus and instantly refreshing with the tang of the salt to bring out its flavour.

In the middle of the afternoon, still at least a couple of

hours from our destination, we made our final stop. Still desperate for drink of any kind we struggled out of the bus. But there was no Pepsi or Coke or fruit to be had here. Down a short slope the bare, flat-roofed buildings that made up this village had no shop and searching for some-one to ask for water, we found a boy of 7 or 8 years old. I asked him in some desperation, 'Pani? pani?' The only Af-ghan word we knew.

He nodded and smiled, he understood. He pointed be-hind a hut, and we raced there in the certain hope of finding a tap to quench our thirst and water for the journey.

There was nothing behind the hut. The dust of the de-sert came right up to the back of the low buildings and for a moment we were clueless. Then we saw it. A small, clear river, flowing silently and at speed around a bend with the ripples catching slivers of green light off the waving rushes on its winding journey through the desert. Did the boy real-ly mean this was to drink? Surely there is a tap somewhere? It was nowhere. This is how water comes to the Afghan villagers. I bent down.

The water, less than two feet deep and just ten feet across, was completely clear, no sediment, and nothing could be carried down the stream in this barren desert. There were shouts from the bus. I unscrewed the top of the bottle and the coolness of the water on my feet surprised me as I dipped the container into the stream. Only then did I see the cluster of small lively minnows engaged in a circle of chase close to the ribbon of reeds that bordered this wa-terway.

The water in the bottle looked clear, nevertheless I put a chlorine tablet in to be sure. The taste of school swim-ming pools didn't do a thing to ease our thirst and my stomach revolted at the chemical.

I never ever thought I could be as thirsty in my life as I was on that one trip, and for many years afterwards at home in England I marveled at the way in which we could turn on a tap to receive lashings of cool water for little cost, yet how many in the world still must dig a well or drink from a muddy stream.

As I had anticipated, the promise of Kandahar by 3pm didn't materialise and the next 3 hours were the longest of my life. An hour from Kandahar, which we reached about 6pm, we began to see tall, lush, green trees and occasional mud-brick houses and increasingly a patchwork of allotment sized field systems of dark brown mud. These were linked together by channels around the edges which were the means by which water was being fed to the green clusters of crops within them.

The shaduf, a bucket on a long pole with a balance at the other end, the kind found on four-thousand-year-old artwork from the tombs of ancient Egypt, was lowered into a small river, probably a tributary of the Arghandab, and lifted easily and swung swiftly across to one of these narrow channels. Here the farmer tipped it so that the channel was quickly awash with the water; the bucket being cast back into the river to fill again.

Then a boy would run ahead of the wave and, with his feet most often, open up a gap in the channel's mud wall to

give the water access to a small area of crops. The water would rush through and another boy or an old man would direct the water along the line of plants. Before the snaking water reached the end of the rows, the first boy was already sealing up the mud wall as another cascading bucket of water moved continuously along the main artery, and further along the channel someone else leapt to open-up another area to be nourished. Against the brown mud, the green plants and trees looked lush, and I feasted my eyes on them, for staring at a dry and barren middle eastern landscape for two weeks had given me a hunger for the colour my European eyes had seen every day of my 24 years; green.

Kandahar began to appear in single-storey dwellings and animal road traffic with its signature antique, home-made carts, traps and wagons with wonky wheels, buckled by heat and wear and probably fashioned by a cartwright long dead. As in Herat, a smoother cart ride for some was found using the wheels from dismembered cars or lorries.

Oblivious to the world around them, these enslaved animals responded reluctantly to stick or whip and swayed under over-laden panniers. Soon, the density of these and occasional motor traffic began to slow our pace. Two storey, flat topped buildings hiding single shops under awnings slid by and market stalls, and hand carts and people in traditional dress and shrouded women following men with children following behind.

Arriving at journey's end just on 6pm, we allowed the Afghans and their women and animals to depart. Then what was left of Ena and I crawled over the last sacks of grain and were pointed to the Palmir Hotel opposite where I was to rest my dehydrated body and aching head. That nightmare was over.

Chapter 7
Kandahar

Herat and Kandahar hotels were austere, grey concrete structures three or four stories high and seemed complimentary to the brutal and barren landscape we had just travelled through. With glassless, shuttered windows and coming in from the heat and white sky filled with desert dust, the interiors were dark with uncarpeted steps and lit by dim electric light day and night. Many back street houses were made of mud brick and the paths between were dust.

'Twenty-five, twenty-five,' snapped the long faced, long robed and turbaned manager as he appeared from the shadows. We paid him twenty each for a shared room on the first floor where my body collapsed onto a low wooden bed. I thankfully and finally rested my spinning head away from the oven heat of the bus.

I slept and was woken an hour later by Ena handing me a glass of ice-cold water. At that moment she was an angel with surely the most beautiful drink of my whole life!

My clothes were stiff with dust and sweat. Later, I went upstairs to take a shower and throwing my shirt onto the floor it failed to collapse but held itself in a kneeling position. The shower was cold, there was no other kind, and after my body, I then tried to wash the day's dust and sweat from my clothes.

Friday night was still hot, but rest was total. We slept and didn't eat again until the next day.

Saturday, and Ena said her goodbyes early, asking if I was going to be OK. I reassured her and she travelled on by bus to Kabul. At the end of another cold shower that morning I seemed to be drying myself for longer than needed, until I realised I was now drying my sweat that was beginning to form again as the heat seeped into the building.

Here in Kandahar the dress of all the people was traditionally Muslim and conservative. If it was not the baggy trousers of the local tribesmen, it was the long robe and hastily wrapped turban for the men, while the few women to be seen were in long, pale blue robes with a head covering that stretched, front and back, down below their waist almost to their knees with the same crocheted visor. As with the bus from Herat, their menfolk were never far away. The hands of these women were never to be seen either and, even when stretched out, were covered by the blue of their gowns like a child's puppet glove.

The hotel was at a junction of main roads by market stalls that were busy with people on this Saturday after Friday's rest and prayers. Occasionally a bus or lorry would pass slowly through the crowds and, as the only European, I drew curious stares.

As I had exited the bus the evening before, struggling with my rucksack and my throbbing head, I had quite literally bumped into an Afghan man, dressed in a long green striped robe and turban who had spoken to me with good English, as I side-stepped out of his way with my bag.

'Hello,' he had said. 'Are you English?' I was in no state to help him or anyone practice their English then. However, on that Saturday afternoon he hailed me with a smile outside the hotel and was determined on conversation.

He introduced himself as Mr. Ahmellah and told me he regularly came to the market just by the hotel to help his friend who owned a stall. Also, he admitted, he wanted to meet any English speakers as they came off the bus, and English people were his favourite. He kindly asked if I had recovered from the journey for he had seen how exhausted I was the previous evening. A not uncommon sight among western travellers, he said. I told him I would be travelling tomorrow to Kabul, and he warned of the same kind of journey, but a little shorter.

On that Saturday evening we talked for an hour of many things, of England and the English language and also of religion too and he explained to me about Muslim traditions. He was also a partner in a commercial business in Kandahar which had begun to do a certain amount of importing and exporting and was hoping to expand. He mentioned mechanical items for all manner of machinery including, inevitably, motor and vehicle spares. 'English is the international language of business,' he assured me, adjusting his makeshift turban. 'Because people in every country can understand it. Iran, Pakistan, India. All understand English.'

I nodded. He waved his hands as he spoke. 'Now we want to import from Europe, maybe England too.' From the small-scale livelihoods evidenced by these family-owned market stalls selling what people had made or grown, this was a comparatively major business he was talking about.

'When you return to England,' he paused, 'please... could you send me a commercial dictionary. My simple English dictionary is not too good for business.'

So that he was not misunderstood, he added, 'The cor-

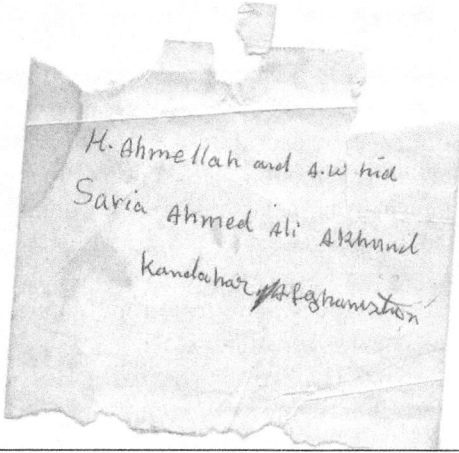

H. Ahmellah and A.W hid
Saria Ahmed Ali Akhund
Kandahar Afghanistan

rect translation of commercial words is very important,' he pleaded with a smile, raising his arms in a gesture of helplessness. I said that I would try, and he immediately took a scrap of paper from his pocket. 'M. Ahmellah and A. Wahid' it read, with his address. This was what passed for a business card in rural Afghanistan in 1974. He pointed to the first name and smiled. 'That is me, Mohammed Ahmellah.' Maybe he had spoken to many English travellers with the same request.

One of the many extraordinary delights of this journey was this mix of characters from different nations you met on the way. At times I was struck by the contrast of the politeness and kindness of inhabitants of strange lands and the unpredictability of many of my fellow tourists, travellers and hippies on the trail.

Saturday night was spent with Australian Barry. Short black hair, not a hippie but a little hyperactive guy whose response to life seemed reflected in his black jeans and T-shirt. He carried with him a large leather bag in which he had scores of sheath knives and pen knives collected at each point in his travels in Southeast Asia, the newly formed Bangladesh and then India.

'Look at this one,' he would say, opening his bag of collectables. He would take out a quality steel blade long enough for the hilt to be in my chest and the tip protruding from my backbone.

'Feel this, go on feel this,' he would insist and thrust another one in my direction. And so as not to stir the potential psychopath in him, I would run my thumb along the edge of the blade and say, 'Wow', and other approving phrases and try not to cut myself. I was grateful that he was travelling the other way - on to Europe - and I maybe understood why he was travelling alone.

Now arrived Hank from Denmark. He and his mate had been travelling with a VW campervan which had broken some part of its clutch somewhere near Kabul. We should remember that those were the days when vehicles were not as reliable as today, and all the vehicles hippies and travellers drove were already years old before the journey.

Before Hank and his friend had set out from Europe they had loaded their van with plenty of spare parts, knowing how difficult it would be to find spares on the trail east. Sadly, this clutch part was not amongst them, and they had been unable to get a replacement in Kabul or Kandahar. They thought their best bet was to try to get back to Iran, a

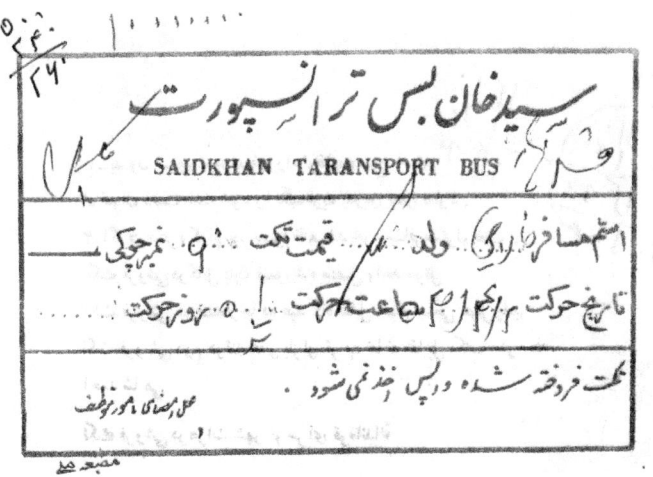

more modern country with strong links to the German car industry and hope to find one there.

Their added problem was that in bringing a vehicle into the country it was registered on the owner's passport and he could not leave the country without it. But the vehicle was not on Hank's passport and so he had to be the one to take a bus trip back to Iran and probably Tehran to find a main dealer, buy the part and travel back to his mate in Kabul.

Christopher was German, and he joined us at the hotel for the night and travelled with me on Sunday up to Kabul. He was tall, dark, slim and bespectacled with a university education and he hoped to train to be a teacher next year. His English was excellent.

It was with some trepidation that I left Kandahar at 6am that Sunday morning on the Saidkhan Taransport (their spelling) Bus, whose journey began outside the hotel, for the price of 90 Afghanis. The sky above was clear blue and cloudless, but the intensity of the heat even at that early hour and the thought of another oven-heated journey, left me wondering again at my own sanity.

Another snub-nosed metal box of a bus loaded with bearded, turbaned and robed or tribally dressed Afghan men. Each, I now saw, with a bag of fruit, tomatoes and cucumbers for the journey; a few young boys were already on the roof with small livestock and luggage of large, white cotton bags. Inside, the women were completely hidden under their blue or black robes and imprisoned behind the fabric grill that hid their eyes. You still had no idea if they were wives or daughters for none were allowed to travel alone. It was as if we were living in parallel worlds with nothing in either language or culture to link us.

Huge sacks of grain were again heaved on board and filled the gangways and Christopher and I clambered over them to get to a bench.

I was basically doing the same journey experience of two days before. This trip to Kabul was 400 kilometers and slightly shorter, therefore, than the last one from Herat. My shirt, washed clean in the shower at the hotel, was now cardboard again by 7am with the desert dust thrown up by other traffic on this much busier road and blown in through the permanently open windows. The heat, the smell of the desert, that every breath sucked moisture out of me, and the never-ending jerking and rattle of the bus on this route made again for a most uncomfortable ride.

The road from Herat had been smooth tarmac all the 450kms to Kandahar. This was a very different road. Kandahar to Kabul was concrete, laid in approx. 30-foot blocks, probably drying before any attempt was made to smooth it over. Like riding a pneumatic drill and, as we drove over the edge of each section, so the bus lurched, juddered and swayed.

We stopped mid-morning at a small village to deliver the post and collect passengers and produce for markets further on and for some refreshment.

Chris and I had chai (small cups of black tea without milk but with sugar) which had been the safe, staple drink from Istanbul. Chai in Asia was considered safe to drink as the water had been boiled. The guarantee of fizzy drinks was that the cans were canned at a factory to western standards. No tap water in Asia could be safely drunk at that time and only fruit that could be peeled before eating should be bought in a market or shop.

Today, I too had a cucumber and two large tomatoes, and while I could not find salt at the market yesterday, the incredible coolness of the cucumber, once peeled, particularly in a desert of over 100°F, was again remarkably refreshing to the mind, mouth and stomach. Christopher found fruit in baskets laid out on the ground under a tree and paid the child squatting in the shade close by.

We stopped at Ghazni about lunchtime and after another cup of chai with Christopher we looked around the market stalls, while the passengers left or refreshed themselves or joined the bus to Kabul. There was the usual fruit to buy or bread and vegetables. However, for some reason my eyes came to rest on a small basket of eggs on one stall. Were eggs good for an unstable stomach? I had no idea if they were boiled or fresh, but the idea came to me that this may be what my still rumbling stomach needed.

Back on the bus, clambering over the sacks of grain to my wooden seat with two of these precious objects in my hand I carefully cleaned and then tapped the end of one of them. They were fresh not boiled. The albumen appeared and I sucked out the egg careful not to spill any. The other egg was soon dispatched in the same way.

Chapter 8
Kabul

We reached Kabul about 3pm, much earlier than I had expected and much to my relief. We were now surrounded by mountains and the heat was much less oppressive. Another Afghan city of low single-story houses and shops which we drove through for about 15 minutes before we stopped at what I thought would be the centre of the city. It was only the bus station on the outskirts. Cars were modern, colourful and plentiful and young Afghans in western dress were calling to us to come in their cars and they would take us to their particular hotel.

> **Please come and stay at**
> **the Green Hotel**
> **and Restaurant**
> **Stereo Music   Garden**
> **Camping**

With a choice, Chris and I went with a young Afghani who showed us a green card.

He spoke some English and so we told him that while we would accept the offer of the lift to see his hotel, we would not necessarily stay at his hotel if it seemed unsuitable. He seemed happy with this, and so we loaded our bags into the boot and drove off.

Some 10 minutes later, he pulled into a small cul-de-sac off what I now know was called amongst the hippies 'Chicken Street' and stopped outside the white-walled enclosure that was the Green Hotel. A garden of thirsty looking green plants and shrubs was the centerpiece with a two-storey building to the left that included the lounge and dining area, while curving around the garden was a covered walkway with small bedrooms off. Chris and I booked a shared room and lay down for an hour. Later we ordered chai from the waiter in a green flowing robe who came to see us in the garden shade.

Ena was also there and had found the companionship of an American youth as they shared a room further down the path. He sat around reading '*The Great Gatsby*', while in the privacy of the compound she hitched her long skirt up to her knees and lounged in the sun. At the back of the compound, I remember, was an area for vehicles and campervans to pull up and stay.

The days in Kabul were still hot by English standards, over 80°F most days. The nights were much cooler, and this was another of the few times on my outward journey that I had to sleep inside my sleeping bag. The bedrooms were bare but for the beds and we were all advised to check our shoes for scorpions before putting them on in the mornings.

One of the great joys of Kabul was that here, for the first time since leaving Istanbul on my hectic journey and living off street food, I found a good supply of western food. There was even a small shop, just a few yards from the hotel, that sold limited flavours of ice cream in a cornet. For someone with a sweet tooth, this was the first place on the journey where I had been able to satisfy it, convincing my healing head and stomach that this was therapy.

Changing my Travellers cheques at an Afghan bank led to a charge of 10Afgs for each cheque which I thought a '*ripoff*'. I began to think that I should have investigated international currency before I started out, for I would have had the cheques in US dollars rather than GB pounds as the exchange rate at that time was far more favourable.

The black-marketeers and moneychangers made a stop at the hotel each morning, walking openly into the garden with its water feature, or into the lounge, and would make themselves available to negotiate a good price for your GB£ or your US$ or Deutschmarks. Also came the drug sellers each day to ask for your needs and to negotiate a price for your relaxing pleasures of presumably, hash or opium.

While the new government had banned the selling and smoking of hashish or marijuana in public areas, there seemed little cooperation from the hotels which regarded themselves as private spaces in this respect.

The hippies that were in the hotel, and many were French while I was there, used the hash or opium in the evenings in the hotel lounge or in their rooms. Sprawled out on the hotel's sofas they invited me to smoke with them and didn't seem to mind my declining, although when offered a smoke it was as casual as if being offered a drink in a pub in England. Most hippies were quite happy to admit they were there for the drugs and to have a good time of living just how they wanted to live. As far as they were concerned there were no western societal restrictions to their chosen lifestyle. They did not see themselves as interfering with the local Muslim culture. In fact, they saw themselves bringing money into a very poor country.

Some hippies had been in Kabul for some weeks, others months and a few, for years. Some had girlfriends they had journeyed with or had decided to pair-off with on the way. But also, a good number of young Europeans and North Americans I met were not interested in the drugs, though they might have tried a puff or two on their travels; they were what I called the tourists and travellers.

Thirty paces from the compound gates at the end of this side street and past, on the right, the ice cream parlour, one came to Chicken Street which stretched away to our left and right. Each side had a raised concrete pavement pathway that ran past the small shops and hotels and businesses, and between that and the grey tarmac road on either side was an open drain for rainwater, now empty for the summer.

At decent intervals, a tree flourished to bring shade to the pavement and every 100 yards or so, sat a policeman dressed in what looked like the faded blue uniform of a First World War Royal Flying Corps pilot; blue peaked cap with thick woollen jacket, made for a cooler European climate, and buttoned-to-the-knee dusty jodhpurs, leggings and boots. In the shade they sat languidly on a chair or stool, brushing away flies and talking to passers-by. Against the wall next to them rested what looked like a British made Lee-Enfield .303 rifle, probably from the same period of history as his uniform.

Other hotels were off this street of low buildings, and just 100 yards away from the Green Hotel on the other side of Chicken Street was the famous Siggi's Hotel. Siggi's, along with The Pudding Shop in Istanbul, was one of the key staging posts of the hippie trail. While all the cheap hotels sold mainly local food and drink to order for residents, this was a hippie hotel and restaurant, owned and run by a German national of that name. Here, the menu was much European from large, breaded wiener-schnitzel with lemon slices, to chicken and lamb dishes or thick and succulent casseroles or various soups with bread rolls. Yes, real bread baked with yeast, not just the local corrugated flatbread.

On several evenings, I sat in Siggi's large square courtyard under a veranda that ran around the edge, facing an overgrown garden of paths and arches, and tasted something European for the first time in 3 weeks. Tea was peppermint and we could help ourselves to as many refills as we wanted by going across the garden to where the pot stood free to all on a table.

When I began this journey, I didn't plan to be back in England much before mid-September, and my hoped-for plan was to get to Kabul overland and then decide what time I still had left and how to use it. But as you can see, I had discovered that I was not a very good traveller in antique, springless buses on bad roads under a roasting sun through desert conditions. My stay in Kabul was therefore a slow recovery from nearly three weeks of hot, fast, incessant and uncomfortable travel. I still had a lot of time to fill before September.

In the garden of the Green Hotel, I met Al. He was a student at Chicago University and was travelling to Pakistan to stay with missionary friends of his family. Al was off on a tour for three days to explore the Panjshir and Bamiyan valleys which, with their lush landscape and scenery and with snow-capped mountain backdrops, were a major tourist attraction. In the Bamiyan were the enormous graven images to Buddah, telling of Afghanistan's Buddhist past. The Mongols had supplanted Buddhism in more recent centuries with Islam. A generation later, the Taliban destroyed these historic images.

Of the dozen or so Brits, French and Americans I met in Kabul, many did the trip and came back amazed. If you were going to spend any time in Kabul then the Panjshir and Bamiyan valleys, about one hundred miles north from the city, seemed to be the main and only tourist attractions.

Afghans had to make a living and like businessmen the world over, they depended sometimes on the naivety of their customers. Andy was a young Brit growing a wispy, blondish beard and had just returned from the Panjshir Valley. The slightly dulled eyes and easy posture he had shown before his trip had been transformed three days later into wide-eyed enthusiasm. He and a friend had been to Bamiyan and camped by the lake. A Tajik tribesman from the village had offered him a deal. Excitement in his every pore, Andy opened his hand to reveal some twenty or so small blue chips of stone that he had had been sold.

I have no idea now of exactly what blue gemstone he claimed these to be, maybe lapis lazuli or sapphires. Nevertheless, Andy had the name and carried the certainty that, back in the UK, they would be worth a lot. I thought there was more light in his eye than these chips reflected, but I was no judge of jewelry. His friend, Bob, was dressed in a sleeveless Afghan coat, one with the wool inside and delicate embroidery around the leather front.

'Look at this,' he insisted, scratching at his beard and pointing to the coat. 'The guy only wanted 200 Afghanis for this! We can sell 'em for loads more in London.'

I had remembered seeing pictures of John Lennon, or was it Paul McCartney, in the New Musical Express in one like this. He looked at his blue-chip friend.

'We're gonna buy ten and take them back with us'.

His blue-chip friend nodded. 'Yeah. 'Then we'll set up in business and come out here and buy loads more,' and their eyes shone at the thought.

It was true that back in the UK these Afghan coats and waistcoats had become a feature of hippie lifestyle. They had an eastern, ethnic credibility that faded, blue, bellbottom jeans with bells around the ankles didn't. But dressed in denims and cheesecloth shirts with scraggly beards and judgement maybe slightly swayed by something they may have inhaled, I nevertheless wished them well. I still also kept faith in the international business ventures of Mr. Ahmellah.

Living in Kabul I had now to decide if I should travel down the Khyber Pass into Pakistan and on to India; or spend more time here before returning to the UK. So far, I had travelled quickly, hardly stopping to take in the cultures and worlds I had been travelling through, but India had always been my hoped-for destination.

I met Cassie (not her real name) one evening in a drugged stupor as I passed her open garden door in the

Green hotel. Incoherent, she seemed to be verbally abusing her poet boyfriend who himself had collapsed on the edge of the low bed, his eyes blinking and unfocussed. This small room was filled with the blue haze and sweet smell of hash. As I looked in, she puked white stuff onto the floor. Then she slowly raised a glance at me.

The next afternoon her skinny frame stepped awkwardly out into the garden, blinking in the strong sunlight. Her hair pulled back, she looked gaunt with sunken eyes as she carefully made her way towards us. Al and I were sat on a bench by the wall. I think she recognized my gingerish beard from the night before as she sat on the grass opposite us.

Over the next hour, she told their story, somewhat haltingly. School sweethearts, they had decided to travel the hippie trail to Kathmandu last autumn in the cooler weather. They had enough money to buy themselves a ten-year-old Bedford dormobile camper. They had taken the journey slowly, enjoying the drugs in Kabul for a couple of months before setting off into Pakistan and India. Finally, in January they got to Kathmandu.

Somewhere thereafter, on the return home, their vehicle had a major mechanical fault that could not be repaired. They dumped the dormobile and decided to make their way home by trying to hitch rides on any passing traffic. I think they hoped other hippie travellers might pick them up in passing. We weren't asking her the details, but there seemed a need in her to tell us. She tried to focus some more.

'Every car and taxi and bus passed us... Eventually a lorry stopped, but the driver spoke no English... He let us climb in the back of his truck and a couple of hours later we stopped at his village... That was as far as he would take us.'

She hesitated, trying to remember the details of a chaotic trip, in her still befuddled mind.

'We slept in a field, afraid of the snakes,' she sniffed. 'In the morning we found the village water pump with a lizard asleep on its hot metal cover. Peter got a stick and...broke its back. Then sliced it open and got rid of the guts and...cut off the head.'

Cassie laughed quietly at the absurdity of it all.

'We found some twigs to light a fire to try and cook it on a long stick.' She closed her eyes and swayed a little at the memory.

As she sat there we knew something was not quite right about this young woman. Surely too young to be caught in the mess life had thrown her, angry at her boyfriend for not getting more money from home, then breaking out in laughter quite inappropriately. One sensed that reason was missing in more senses than one. Perhaps it was something she had smoked.

Cassie had been no more than a glancing memory over the years. But nearly twenty years later, she appeared in one of our offices. She didn't recognize me; my ginger beard had long gone. I did recognize her. Now late thirties she looked grey, lined and fifty; makeup trying to disguise the dark circles around her eyes. and life had taken its toll on her.

At the interview stage she had heightened anxiety that reminded me of her conduct in Kabul. Her pupils were pin-points. She presented herself unkempt with an unsmiling demeanor and the panel were undecided about her suitability for what was a demanding role. Without revealing my prior knowledge of her I argued against her employment. However, the area boss, Brian, said to us, 'We've got no choice. No-one else wants the job. The post has to be filled.'

Cassie turned out to be all the nightmare that I had feared. Her husband was still the same Peter the poet, now a carpenter.

After seventeen years, life was still pretty much the same for them. They were broke and penniless. They lived in a ruin of a cottage on the moors that Peter was meant to be doing up for them. He was tired of supporting her while she had been at university and wanted some quality of life. If she failed in this job he would divorce her, she told me. In conversation she said, without a blink of an eye, that they smoked cannabis in the evenings with their two teenage sons. Unlike some hippies, she never gave up the habit.

Months later, Brian came to her office for her review.

'Who chose her?' Cassie's supervisor demanded. 'Cassie is totally unsuitable. She has no insight, compassion or emotional intelligence. She has a complaining spirit about any work given to her. She has massive mood swings, uppers and downers, and the evidence is that she's a manic depressive.' Unknown to them Cassie was listening just the other side of the door.

The long-term psychological effects of the use of cannabis, not so much known about in the 1970s but re-searched now, were very apparent in Cassie's conduct at work; unpredictable mood swings, sudden bouts of anxiety, paranoia and periods of listlessness and deep depressions. Wreckage from a life in drugs that she was now passing on to the next generation in her family and which, shortly afterwards, exploded in her workplace.

Chapter 9
Kabul to Pakistan

I had decided that I would leave Kabul for India on the Sunday, and so on the Friday I went to buy my coach ticket. Yes, this one was to be a coach. Consternation as they re-layed to me at the Pakistan Road Transport Corporation's ticket office by the hotel's crossroads, that the earliest I could leave would be Monday, and only if there were any seats left. Close by, I tried the Afghan Bus Co. too; same answer.

Now the reason I needed to leave on the Sunday was that I didn't want to change any more Travellers cheques into Afghanis as this would be a useless currency in Pakistan. And another day would mean a Travellers cheque would have to be changed. This was how tight my money was.

Getting a coach ticket out of Kabul was something of a ripoff, as each bus company apparently always claimed there was a three-day waiting list for tickets into Pakistan. 'They just want you to stay and spend some more money here', the hippies sighed. Looking back, you could understand the reasoning.

Ice cream helped cool my temper. Later that afternoon I returned to the Road Transport Corporation's ticket office and stood in the queue for Monday's ticket. In front of me were a smart hippie couple; for him a black, trimmed beard, beads and a colourful long kaftan shirt; and she in the same beads and full-length flowered cotton dress. They gazed dreamily into each other's eyes, oblivious of the world around them. They wanted to stay longer in Kabul. Amazingly, they were handing back the tickets they had bought to leave Kabul on Sunday. Oh joy! I happily took one.

By Saturday Al had arrived back from his trip to the

Panjshir Valley much enthused by what he had seen of the giant Buddha statues. He declared himself a Christian but was impressed with the size of the statues and the devotion of the sculptors for the creation of the gigantic figures.

'Why don't you become a Buddhist,' I mused.

'Because it's a 'do' religion. And I'm not into 'doing'. Jesus is freedom,' he proclaimed. Al explained.

'All other religions are 'do' religions. They are about having rituals and prayers to say and do; visiting sacred sites, often praying to images of stone or plaster or turning a prayer wheel, rather than praying in words yourself and genuinely meaning them in your heart. It is these things that apparently make you acceptable to those gods.'

'Christianity is about change on the inside. And it's the one and only 'done' religion,' he explained. 'Jesus died to take away my sins. Mortal, sinful me could never please an almighty all-powerful God. Jesus' sacrifice alone is enough to make me acceptable to God. Jesus is about relationship not rituals.'

I told him of my occasional work sending sacks of educational material to a Christian organization in Bombay. Al had also bought a ticket to travel to Pakistan on the Sunday with the same transport company.

I recently found a postcard I had written to my brother Brian from Kabul.

'My shared hotel room costs 15p per night; peaches 1/2p each and a good meal comes at 20p. However, the water is undrinkable, Coca Cola has a high tax on it and the toilet thinks the problem over before flushing! I have now got the best part of a beard not having shaved for three weeks. But I expect in the heat of the Pakistan plains I will have to shave it off. By the way, when you go abroad take your money in US dollars or Deutschmarks. Inflation seems to hit our wet, limp pound even in hot dry Asia. My bus ride to Peshawar in Pakistan next Sunday will cost me just 60p!

From Erzerum in Turkey to Tehran to Kabul there are streets and streets of small shops all selling exactly the same fruit and food as their neighbours, with occasionally other items of clothing or shoes, but somehow all managing to make a living.'

Once he knew I was leaving, the young manager of the hotel, Mohammed, came to me as I sat with a tray of chai in the garden writing some notes for my diary. Very politely, he asked if I would write on the back of some of his hotel cards some form of recommendation for the hotel. This, so he could show them to people that they met off the Kandahar bus, in the same way that I had been met by them a week before.

I put together a form of words, for the hotel could not be faulted and compared most favourably to those airless, dark and featureless concrete structures in Herat or Kandahar. Here in his walled garden compound, with ground floor rooms, with a café service if required, there was music with a cassette player and speakers ('with two speakers to make it stereo,' reminded Mohammed). All day he would play from the lounge everything from Pink Floyd, The Who, Rod Stewart, to the Beach Boys to be heard over the garden area.

I often wished afterwards that I had charged him for

my recommendations, for I think my persuasive words and phrases must have helped give him a good income - at least until the Russians came.

Sunday 30th June and the Road Transport Company of the North-West Frontier Province of Pakistan had advised us to be at their offices for 7.30am with our 100 Afgs ticket, for departure at 8am for Peshawar in Pakistan. Al and I and a score of other hippies and adventurers and some Pakistani men, who had been doing business in Kabul, queued at the offices of the bus company where a dusty ten-year-old coach stood ready to take us first to Jalalabad, eighty miles away and a three-hour journey.

Have you read *'The Kite Runner'* or *'A Thousand Splendid Suns'*; books by Khalid Hosseini? The first is a novel of Afghanistan starting from 1975 following the relationship of two boys as they grow up. The second book follows the disturbing life of the two Muslim wives of one man and their life in Kabul under Taliban rule.

At one point the two desperate wives try to escape their intolerable life and attempt to purchase bus tickets to Peshawar. But they are not allowed to do this simple task. They need a man to purchase the tickets from the official and a man to travel with them.

As I read the book, I realised that I and many other

hippie trail travellers had just such a ticket, purchased so cheaply and easily a generation before Taliban rule.

First, we followed the river, cutting its way from the height of Kabul and, as the torrent disappeared, to our left appeared a precipitous drop of many hundreds of feet to the valley floor below. The two-lane road that gave Kabul access to the East and to Pakistan and India had been dug into the side of these cliffs like a scar, and we could see slow movement of occasional traffic miles ahead as the road wound itself around the edges of these cliffs.

I loved history and before I came on this trip I had read about Lord Elphinstone's 16,000 tragic troops and camp-followers in the winter of 1842. They paid the price of his military bungling and the political incompetence in London and Delhi, by being picked off by sharpshooter Afghan tribesmen from the mountains when the British politics in Kabul failed.

Only a handful survived to get to the safety of the Jalalabad garrison, and captured Indian sepoys became slaves of their new Afghan masters. On hearing the news in London, the British prime minister is said to have had a heart attack. Later that year the sepoys were released when the British sent a punitive force of troops to punish the Afghans.

Years later I would inherit from a distant relative a campaign medal dated 'Cabul 1842', on a much-faded rainbow ribbon of the British East India Company, who had ruled India at that time. Also came an Afghan silver goblet, slightly battered. A London jeweler confirmed the strange hallmarks on the goblet as being from 'the British India border with Afghanistan in the 1840s'. Probably a looted souvenir from this punitive campaign. Ensign C.A. Reid of the 58th Bengal Native Infantry in the distant family had beaten me to Kabul by 132 years. I dread to think what 'punitive' measures he might have been involved in during the summer of 1842.

Fifteen years later in 1857, now Colonel Reid, he had managed to escape from the massacres of that year's Indian Mutiny. (The Mutiny is now known in India as the First War of Independence.) Ordered to fire the new Enfield cartridges in their rifles, the Indian sepoys refused. The cartridges were covered with paper that had to be torn off with the teeth. Muslim soldiers believed the paper was greased with pig fat and Hindus believed it was cow fat; handling the paper would have been religiously abhorrent to each group. This and other strongly felt injustices led to the uprising.

The family story handed down through the years, told of Colonel Reid being unwell on the morning his Bengal troops paraded at the barracks at Meerut, when the Indian sepoy mutineers turned on and killed their British officers.

Hearing the commotion from his sick bed, he leapt out of the window, grabbed a horse and bolted to safety.

His eighteen-year-old grandson Eric was a Lieutenant in the Hampshire regiment and was not so lucky in 1918. His regiment records show that; *'A' Company went up the line (to the Front) on Monday 25th March. Following a German artillery bombardment on Friday morning 29th March, 'A' Company could not be found.'*

Eric's name is carved on the Arras Memorial. He has no known grave.

Even in 1974 there were still dangers for travel on this road for people in vehicles of their own, and two US women had been raped and killed here a month or two before my journey. There were tales of other lone travellers who had simply disappeared.

As I edit this book in December 2022, I read in the paper today of the release from prison in Nepal of the 'Serpent'. The Frenchman called Charles Sobhraj, who was convicted of at least six murders along the hippy trail from 1975 to 1985, but who was thought to have killed at least twenty people in total. His mainly American and Canadian victims were drugged and killed as far apart as Afghanistan, India, Thailand, Turkey, Nepal, Iran and Hong Kong during the 1970s and 80s.

Sobhraj was given the name Serpent for his ability to slither out of the clutches of the police, something he would end up doing for years. Did our paths cross in the summer of 74? On his release this month he told reporters, "I have a lot to do. I have to sue a lot of people". In 2021, the BBC and Netflix produced a drama series called *The Serpent,* based on the story of Sobhraj's alleged killings.

Frank, from the USA, was a wide, chunky guy of 45+ with an extended belly being supported by a thick, leather belt who, in spite of the heat, dressed in tight-fitting US army fatigues and military style boots. He boasted he had travelled the world and was now, 'Doin' the India trip, man'. It was not just his age that made him stand out from the crowd; nor that he wore his US citizenship so proudly and noisily, but what he carried around his waist.

The thick, brown leather army belt was hung with large rings of keys that he had probably collected everywhere he travelled. He had no item to lock, and he gave no explanation for them, and we asked for none, for the hippie trail accepted people as they were. And at least this was a safer collection than the knife guy in Kandahar. As strangers to each other we were all anonymous and for most of us our lives only touched for a few moments. Frank never made mention of the keys or reached to use one, but they must have added another stone to his already bulky weight.

Frank was noisy, loud and complaining on the whole trip and his voice could be heard everywhere on the coach. In truth, in this respect he was not unlike a lot of the US hippies, which was why locals from Turkey to India on the hippie trail liked much more the politer English and European travellers.

Frank had brought with him a very large, green and yellow striped watermelon that he struggled to carry under one arm with his large, leather bag across his other shoulder. Our tickets, we had learned, didn't include payment for luggage. Bags in the boot of the bus were extra.

'Whadaya mean, you want me to pay extra for the watermelon?' he had complained to the driver's assistant. 'It stays on the seat!' he glared.

We stopped later that morning at Jalalabad where the coach pulled into a shopping and market area. We disembarked, looked around at the market stalls of mainly locally grown food and found a large area of tables and chairs and all sat down and ordered chai.

Key Man took a large jack-knife from his bag and proceeded to cut open the watermelon to reveal the succulent rose-pink and white flesh. He generously insisted that we share it with him and in the heat he sliced and watched us as we ate. This, my first taste of watermelon. It was surprisingly cool and so refreshing and nourishing as the juice dripped over my chin and hands, but the multitude of black pips interrupted the full enjoyment.

After Jalalabad, the Khyber Pass was a thrilling descent into the plains of Hindustan. With a sheer drop to our left, we could see thousands of feet below us it seemed, and far in the distance, the dense haze forming over the flat landscape of the Pakistan plains in the heat of the summer day. We had been relatively cool in Kabul; the weather had been like the best of an English summer, but nothing oppressive.

Again, we could see the road ahead for some miles snaking across the sides of the mountains, clinging to the rock face, suspended it seemed by unseen hands. Our ears popped as we drove down towards the steaming pale-green plains now appearing, and there was a sense of our mountain and plateau world ending as we looked into our oppressively sweaty future.

The riverbed that journeyed with us part of the way, was surprisingly deep and rapid as the ice on the mountain tops melted in the summer heat. Every few hundred feet we descended we began to feel the rising temperature and the humidity becoming like an unwanted guest at a party. As we approached the border, twisting and turning on what was becoming one winding, narrow road between the rock faces of the Pass, now rising vertically above us, the driver's assistant walked up and down the coach insisting, 'No smoke. No smoke!' He pushed the windows open because the smell of hash being smoked was everywhere.

'If Pakistan border guard smell smoke they will come on bus and search your bags and refuse entry,' he snapped. He met with complaints.

'Oh, come on, man, give us a break,' was the common feeling, but eventually he got compliance.

The border post was wedged in at the foot of the mountain pass and was advertised by a large sign. We stopped at a long concrete block of a building on the right where, to my surprise, a large number of Afghani men in tribal dress and Pakistanis in western dress were waiting for us outside the building. This was the black market in foreign exchange.

They surrounded the coach as we unpeeled ourselves from the seats, and all the time as we made our way to the offices, they got in our way, tugged at our sleeves offering a good price for US dollars or Deutschmark's or GB pounds. How they got away with it in the full sight of officials, soldiers and police I didn't understand. I was simply a naive westerner.

We made our way up the steps and inside to find a long desk the length of the building but partitioned halfway. We gave our passports to the Afghan officials simply to be stamped as leaving their country, and we backed over to the far side of the room beyond the long, partitioned desk to await the return of our travel documents. Al, my travelling companion, disappeared and came back a few minutes later.

'There's a guy over there on his way back to the UK. He's from that Christian organisation you sent those sacks to.'

I was amazed. I found him. His name was Patrick. We talked and I told him that I had been packing books and education materials and sending them off to an office in Bombay. He confirmed who he worked for and immediately wrote their Delhi office address in my notebook and encouraged me to visit them; Gautam Nagar, next to the New India Hospital. He even drew a map for me. I had had no idea in my head exactly what I was going to do when I got to India. Now I had a plan.

Chapter 10
Journey to Lahore

Now on the Pakistan side of the building with our passports returned, our baggage was searched again before we were allowed back on the coach to continue our journey. The heat outside was akin to a Turkish steam bath. Inside the coach, we were in the oven that was in the Turkish steam bath. By now you must feel that I should not be complaining.

Outside, we passed miles upon miles of open fields of crops with solitary farmers or peasants at work stripped to the waist in their dhotis, and villages of dirt roads and low buildings. Countless people walking with loads on backs or heads or on bicycles; colourfully decorated but overloaded lorries groaning in low gears, and the tuk-tuk taxis that seemed to be everywhere.

I now sat close to two chubby, bespectacled young American males, who from their clothes were neither hippies nor travellers, but who seemed to confidently and loudly have a good grasp of the new world order. The order that put the USA as the most powerful and important country in the world and them as its ambassadors for youth. Both had fathers working at the embassy in Pakistan, they said. They were tourists, not travellers.

They asked me what I thought of the roads I had travelled on in Afghanistan. They smiled at each other knowing, I think, what I was going to say. I said the road from Herat to Kandahar was excellent, tarmac and smooth; but the road from there to Kabul was rough without reason. 'Why couldn't they make the two roads the same?' I demanded.

They laughed. 'Yeah, you know why? The old king of Afghanistan a few years ago wanted modern roads to link his cities. Wanting to be seen as being even-handed, he asked the US and the Ruskies. The Russians immediately said they would build the one from Kabul to Kandahar. So, we built the other one.'

'Great,' I said, 'but why was that Russian road so rough?'

'Oh man!' said the other looking past me out of the window. I sensed I was about to be patronized.

'The Russians will one day invade Afghanistan and so they laid a 3ft deep concrete road all the way from Kabul to Kandahar so their tanks and tank transporters can just zip down to the south in a day.'

His friend jumped in. 'That was why the US built the other road from Kandahar to Herat in the northeast and made it of tarmac. Yup, it's smooth all right, but put a tank on it and it will just churn up. A tank transporter will destroy it too. It's made just for buses and cars. When the Russians invade, they will never be able to conquer the whole country.' They smiled at their nation's cleverness.

I had thought I was well up on world affairs; heavens, in the UK I read the Guardian newspaper. I smiled politely, it seemed an interesting idea but a bit overblown and a touch far-fetched, I mused silently. I casually dismissed their idea for the next 5 years, until December 1979 when the Russians did invade Afghanistan. Now I wonder if those guys ended up working for the US State Department. Was one of them a young Donald Rumsfeld?

There was nothing in Pakistan or India, that could not be carried on the back of a bicycle. If the cyclist stood up then his wife could ride on the seat with a baby; and the pannier at the back could include another person; four on a bike. Milk churns, a box of chickens, a goat, a car's major engine parts, trunks, suitcases, bags and tools; but most of all women being peddled by their husbands, elderly fathers peddled by daughters, children peddling parents. How to move a double size mattress? Balanced on the head of the cyclist with the boy behind on the pannier holding it straight. All the bikes had the 'sit up and beg' attitude.

Around six in the evening we pulled into Peshawar and here Al and I said goodbye. He was off to stay with some missionaries who lived in a village close to the town. Several of us, including Frank the Key Man, went off to find food and refreshments at a café where I had some vegetable soup and ice-cold Pepsi Cola. Enough to keep body and soul together.

Pepsi, Coca Cola, Tango or 7Up were still the staple drink of most travellers along with chai (served with hot milk and sugar in India and Pakistan) and were to be found everywhere at almost every stall, for the heat sucked the life and energy from the locals too. Interestingly, Persil and Omo, products used in the UK for clothes washing, were still available in every town along the hippy trail. Not as powders for machines. Now as large bars of soap to rub onto the clothes.

Some of our travelling companions wanted to rest here from the heat of the journey so far. But a few of us thought that with the evening coming on we would be better suited to travel in the cool, overnight. We booked seats on a single-decker bus, a coach was not an option, from Peshawar to Lahore. This was to be a journey over 300 miles, and nearly twelve hours of travel, for just 15 Rupees.

Was this one the worst journey imaginable? The night didn't in any way cool the air and the humidity remained very high. Families and businessmen filled the bus which made all the stops in the main towns as we travelled making it a very slow journey. In darkness we passed through Rawalpindi and over a river bridge where under floodlights soldiers stood guard. The Pakistani roads were rough, even though tarmacked, and because if this and the heat, it was impossible on the benches to get any sleep. All the windows were open, but the blasts of hot air only added to our thirst. By the time we reached Lahore at 6am the next morning, Monday the first of July, our sweat and dust of the road had again created khaki cardboard shirts for us all.

Chapter 11
Lahore

Monday 1st July: Lahore at last and, off the bus with great relief, we found we were in the centre of a large market area with saloon cars of all kinds and tuk-tuk taxis lined up. We asked for hotels and were met with blank stares. It appeared that this was one part of the journey where there were very few cheap hotels because most hippies didn't stay. With the more appealing city of Amritsar with the Hindu holy site of the Golden Temple just a few miles away across the Indian border, they simply travelled on through and left this featureless city behind.

Then a bearded Sikh caught our eye and told us of the Tourist Inn Hotel. It was the only one on offer, so we climbed into his horse-drawn four-wheeled carriage. The hotel was set on the corner of two streets and seemed large, compared to the pension style hotels in Istanbul. It had a wide concrete staircase leading up to large, airy rooms, bare of all furniture except beds.

My travelling companions from Peshawar had been two American girls travelling together, with Richard from the UK aged about 20. We threw ourselves down onto the beds that were little more than elderly, wooden bed frames strung across with thin, hairy sisal rope – there were no mattresses. Extremely hot, exhausted and very uncomfortable, the bed was like being caught in a net. I was unable to sleep. I heaved myself up from this cradle an hour later and took a small tuk-tuk taxi to the Central Post Office. There at the Poste-Restante desk I picked up some letters from home.

I now looked around for somewhere to eat and wondered, as I examined these expensive restaurants, which one I dare enter in my cardboard shirt and dust powdered complexion. They all seemed uninviting, and I couldn't blame them. While I drew the curious stares of some passersby, I persisted in my search until I came across a small restaurant with a display of coloured lights over the door and labelled, 'Pejo Snacks, 47 The Mall, Lahore'.

I pulled open the door to find the café modern and bright. But what hit me immediately was the cool air conditioning. Wow! Such a welcome surprise. Britain in the 1970s had no air conditioning in any building I had been in. I had spent one summer holiday working in Appleby's food wholesaler in Bristol, and the best place to be that summer of 1969 was stacking the cheese or butter boxes in the office-sized freezer.

Now this was the coolest I had been for weeks, and my body drew the cool air into every pore. The shock of pleasure, even joy, to my system was enormous and I sucked the air to my lungs gratefully. I gave a friendly nod to the owner and found a seat at the back of the empty café. He allowed me time to sit and examine his menu before coming over to take my order.

Whatever he thought of my physical condition he gave no hint, but as the café was empty he probably appreciated the trade. I ordered a vegetable soup and lime juice because I recognised these things on the menu. You may notice I ate a lot of vegetable soups. It meant I needn't worry what the meat content was, and it would have been heated to a very high temperature at least or boiled. This cost me 4.5 Pakistani Rupees and the exchange rate was about 23 Rupees to the UK pound.

No, I was not being very adventurous with food. The dreaded Delhi Belly could be experienced all along the hippy trail long before you got to Delhi.

'With chilis or not?' The smiling face of the café owner was asking.

'Oh... no, er... no chilis, thankyou,' I insisted, to

please my stomach. With the cool air and the food and drink I was soon feeling halfway to restored.

The owner moved over to start a conversation with me telling me the temperature outside was probably over 120°F today. The friendliness, good price and the cool air brought me back here each day of my stay in this city.

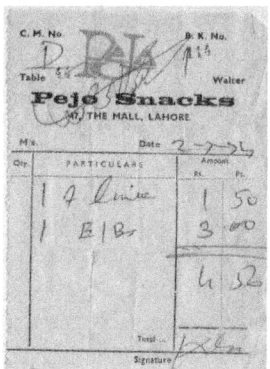

I returned to the hotel and tried to get some sleep on the rope bed. Yet the heat in the concrete all around was determined to rob me of that. I rested, with the shouts and calls of bustling crowds in the street and market below going about their business.

But my day was not over yet. I had seen from the café, the Lahore YMCA. I had stayed in Bristol at the YMCA immediately before my departure and had been given a letter of recommendation from the manager there to any YMCA I went to on my travels. I decided I would go and introduce myself.

The Pakistani manager, Mr. Albert, was friendly and interested to see the letter and appreciative of interest from across the world. He invited me to meet Rev. Sidney Igguldon, a Scotsman who was the minister of St Andrew's Church of North India situated close by.

I spent an hour in the company of this warm-hearted Scotsman talking about my travels, and he of his work over many years as a missionary priest. I felt much refreshed in my spirit from our time together and he wished me well for my onward journey. But also invited me to have a meal with him and his wife tomorrow, Tuesday evening.

Tuesday morning, I found myself in a predicament. I didn't have enough Pakistani money to get a taxi to a bank and decided that I should have to walk in the heat to find one. Keeping to the shadows and taking a main road I thought would be the answer, I found myself later near the railway station with not a bank in sight. I searched the roads, asked the shopkeepers but had no joy.

'What is happening in Northern Ireland?'

A well-rounded, rough-bearded shopkeeper standing in front of his shop guarding his many boxes and displays of fruit and vegetables decided to challenge me about the most intractable problem in the western hemisphere. Business was slack. Time to tease a Brit. He lifted his shirt and scratched his belly.

'What are you Christians doing killing each other?' he challenged again, wiping a hand under his armpit this time. We didn't introduce ourselves.

'Well,' I began, struggling to find a set of words that might explain Britain's major social and political headache. 'Er… It's not really Christians killing each other.'

His large hand wiped now at his bushy moustache, and he scratched his week's growth of beard. 'Yes yes yes!' he insisted raising his voice. 'Catholic and Protestant killing each other. Why?'

I tried again. 'Catholic and Protestant are just names of different groups of people, different communities,' I said. 'They don't go to church. They are not believers.'

'They are very bad,' he snapped. 'Christians killing each other.' He turned and sloped back into his shop.

I stepped off the pavement into the street to be stopped by a young man whose paler skin and blue eyes gave his origins away. John Morgan introduced himself as Anglo-Pakistani and wanted to tell me about himself, pleased as he was that I was English and not American. I was to find that Brits over many generations in the subcontinent had left their seed and DNA in its people.

John was about my own age, friendly and engaging and asked me about England, naming some London landmarks and politicians. His English father had been a Major in the army, and I think he hungered to speak to English people and identify with them. Often mixed-race Anglo-Pakistani people could be viewed suspiciously by their Pakistani countrymen who had shaken off the shackles of colonialism a generation ago. Where did the loyalties of mixed-race people really lie? I was to find it was to be the same in India, too.

Inevitably, John had a story to tell of some discrimination and poverty, but he was so helpful to me in guiding me through the busy streets to a bank that I gave him some Rupees for his help and many thanks. I had already had the experience of being lost in the city of Erzurum and the crowded streets here in Lahore with no map or idea of direction had not been a comfortable experience.

Lunchtime, and I now introduced Richard and the two girls from the USA, Sue and Sandy to the delights of Pejo Snacks. Like nearly all the Americans I had met so far they were chubby, likeable and voluble.

Sandy, with dark cropped hair came from a small town near Chicago where she lived in a very large house with her parents and four brothers. I guess if you are the only daughter in a household of boys you learn to stand your ground pretty well anywhere. She told us they all had cars, all kept in garages of their own, and when the parents wanted to speak to any of their offspring they had to use an intercom system because their house was huge.

This all seemed extraordinary to Richard and myself who, like most Brits, lived in terraced or semi-detached houses or in flats, probably the size of just two of her brothers' garages. Real Estate was her Dad's business which she explained as being like an estate agent in the UK.

Sandy, who had already spent a month in London, didn't gush about the politeness of our policemen as Americans tended to do in those days, but did gush about the boutiques on the King's Road in Chelsea and the clothing delights of Carnaby Street. She and her friend Sue had met up in London through mutual friends and both having the idea of the hippie trail decided to travel together.

They too were travellers rather than hippies and were more than excited at the prospect of seeing the full moon over the Taj Mahal on the coming Thursday 4th July; American Independence Day. Both girls were to leave for Amritsar tomorrow morning to meet their deadline.

Getting back to the hotel, I noticed a wind beginning to batter the shutters and a sky of grey, flat cloud. Through the afternoon the wind grew much stronger and it threw the dust off the roads and alleyways up in whirlwinds into the sky to beat the skin and sting the eyes. Then the sky turned yellow.

I was not sure quite what the endgame of this weather might be, yet the offer of supper with Sidney Igguldon at St Andrew's vicarage still appealed. At just on 6pm as I crossed the street to get a taxi, the wind, without warning, suddenly strengthened to an almighty roar and rain came bulleting down from the sky battering onto the roofs and earth. In a moment the streets were empty.

I had been exactly halfway across the road from the hotel at this point and, unable to return, I took shelter under an awning opposite. In awe of nature's punishing wrath at my world I was initially unaware, a few minutes later, of a door opening behind me. When I turned around, a small, smiling, bespectacled man of about thirty-five silently beckoned me inside. He had something to be proud of. And he wanted to show a westerner.

I found myself in his workshop-cum-factory. Around, above and beyond me was the hum of power and activity as an unseen generator turned a drive shaft which in turn powered black rubber and fabric belts, six inches wide and up to fifteen feet long, that drove the machines to power his wood-turning and carpentry workshop. Surely these rickety and wobbling belts, that looked like something from a Heath Robinson cartoon, could not be that productive? Yet the wood dust that lay inches deep on the windowsills and in every corner where activity had not removed it, spoke otherwise.

Carefully crafted on his machines by himself and his three fellow workers, ornate chairs, tables and other furniture stood at one side ready to be taken away from this dusty environment and the finishing touches of polish to be applied and to be made ready for his traders to sell. Separately, a collection of chair and table legs were waiting to be bought and taken by other furniture makers.

The owner, Hasim, kindly offered me chai, and as we walked around the workshop his machines hummed, the belts drove the lathes and the shavings dropped to the floor and the dust took to the still warm, untroubled air. Outside the rain lashed buildings, cascaded off roofs and made rivers of streets.

Hasim talked quietly about his business and his desire to bring his young son into it when he was older. He asked about my travels and said how he would very much like to visit London and England at some time in the future. He said he had great respect for the British. Now, nearly fifty years after my travels, as I write in the third decade of the twenty first century, it could be difficult for Pakistanis or

British people to imagine anyone could say anything other than bad things about British colonialism.

With the rainstorm still building up to full force outside this was a generous and kindly man, and I showed all the appreciation he deserved for his ingenuity and cleverness and craftmanship with such simple and basic resources. Hasim also explained that this weather was a cyclone, quite typical at this time of year, and the Indian Ocean equivalent of a hurricane in the western world.

None of the taxi cabs were operating and so I had to cancel my evening out with Sidney Igguldon. Later, having squelched my way back to the hotel, I stood under a shelter on the roof and watched the yellow sky continue to bowl down the rain with tremendous force over the rooftops of the deserted community. Close by, a slender metal telegraph pole swayed in the wind almost down to a 90-degree angle, and telephone and power cables which criss-crossed the street in an incoherent spider's web were thrashed against each other. I went to bed hungry.

The following day, Wednesday, the cyclone was gone. The air was noticeably cooler, fresher and cleaner now that the dust in the air had been picked up by the rain and hammered into the ground again. People were surveying the damage to the huts in the market area, and to my amazement the rooftop telegraph pole was still intact.

I took the tuk-tuk taxi to the vicarage and apologised to Sidney for my failure to turn up the previous evening. He smiled and said he was not surprised. He had lost part of the church roof last night, and a 6ft high wall over 40 feet long had also collapsed in the winds of up to 140mph. He said the newspapers were reporting eleven people in the city having been killed by the cyclone. He wished me well for the onward journey. The American girls, Sue and Sandy, and Richard had left yesterday, and I wondered if they had made it to the border and into Amritsar in safety.

Lovely Ena, my saviour from Kandahar, was again a solitary traveller on the trail, and arriving at the hotel that afternoon she immediately decided she wanted to explore the market.

'Ever tasted a mango?' she said to me. 'What are they like?' I had no idea and even in upcountry Kenya we didn't have this exotic fruit.

'I'm going to get us some.' She disappeared. Within minutes she returned somewhat breathless, brushing her mousy blonde hair aside as she looked back over her shoulder to the street.

'Come with me,' she ordered, and with no further explanation something inside me told me she needed me to return her previous favour.

As soon as we hit the street, Pakistani men of all ages

seemed to focus themselves on her. It was not that their staring was obvious, for it was not.

But it was immediately apparent from their change in behaviour and direction of travel that she was the focus of their interest. No-one pointed at her or made her the focus of an intrusive gaze, but on the sidewalk, although their eyes were fixed ahead, many deliberately adjusted their path to come as close to Ena as they could. Other men casually crossed the street, staring fixedly ahead, simply so that they could try to get as close as possible and in one or two cases 'accidentally' brush past her bare arm.

Ena was wearing a long dress, but her blonde head and forearms were uncovered. Despite my attempts to walk behind, in front and beside her at all times at least two men touched more than her arm as they passed at close quarters, to her great annoyance. The stall holder was agog too, as she searched in her purse to pay him for the mangos and other fruit, and he made sure he touched her hand as she passed the money over. Even in Herat, Kandahar or Kabul she had not been treated like this.

Suddenly, there was a shout from in front of us and people were leaping to the side, until we were the only ones to face, immediately in front of us, the scything horns of the biggest domesticated creature found outside Africa; a water buffalo, the domesticated hippo of Hindustan. Like some drunk on a late Saturday night, this ton of a creature with its wild eyes moved unsteadily yet remorselessly up between the market stalls, straining forward its enormous black head with its pink tongue lashing over its frothing white lips, shoulders pumping like pile-drivers and hillsides of hips swaying in a motion to fill the alleyway.

Nothing it seemed could stop this creature and a young boy ran beside its swaying flanks waving a stick and shouting ahead unable to get past the swaying head of horns. The buffalo's feet seemed incongruously small to its massive size.

Back at the hotel, the mango was not to our taste; unripe, fibrous and the stones too large. Yet even now the taste of mango takes me back to Ena, the buffalo and the street market.

Gino was Italian and he spoke not a word of English and had no idea how to go and buy food. How he had managed to travel so far on the trail with so little English and survive I had no idea. But I did take him back into the market where he bought some peaches, fruit and food to satisfy his gnawing hunger.

Did I tell you no one took a camera on this route? I lied. A year after my journey I was staying in north London and met with Andrew who, with his childhood sweetheart, had set off for India one year before me. They had been married for just one year when she had died in the dreadful London Underground rail accident that had shaken the nation in 1975. When I met him he was still grieving and his feelings were raw, but when he heard I had been on the hippie trail he searched for a photo to show me.

'Recognise it,' he asked? 'Of course,' I said. The grey and white concrete structure of three stories stood at the corner of two streets. 'Tourist Inn Hotel, Lahore'.

That Thursday morning, Gino and I and three others from the hotel took the bus to the border just a few miles away for 80 paise each. Most of the telegraph poles that lined the route had been blown down overnight. Then I noticed that they were only rods of wood about 12ft long and a few inches in diameter and were probably free standing and could simply have been placed on the ground, as the storm began, to avoid damage.

The Pakistan and Indian Wagha border buildings were separated by a few hundred yards of narrow tarmac road which provided a no-man's-land of huge plane trees that must have seen over one hundred years of Hindustan history. Now they sucked some of the oppressive heat out of the air and provided shade to the tourists.

Relations between the two countries had been difficult since the creation of Pakistan in 1948, and just two years ago the two countries had been at war over the independence of East Pakistan as it became an independent country now called Bangladesh. At that time no passenger aircraft from India were allowed over Pakistani airspace.

It was while on the Pakistan side of the Wagha border, going through the formalities, that the clerk, claiming to have mislaid his pen, indicated to me to borrow mine that I was using for form filling. It was a Parker pen given to me when I had left my last teaching post. He used it quickly, asking me questions as he looked at my passport and then waved me on, irritably. The questions and the over 100-degree heat were enough of a distraction, and it was only when I was halfway across the open no-man's land under the plane trees that I realised my loss. But I had no inclination in the heat to return. Could I remember to collect it on my way back in a couple of months?

Chapter 12
India

In the immigration office on the Indian side, us Brits were quickly through, but Gino inexplicably didn't have a visa and had to endure the walk back into Pakistan and bus back to Lahore. How had he managed to get so far on the hippie trail when in every new country he would have needed a new visa?

A taxi offered to take the rest of us the few miles into Amritsar for 10 Indian Rupees each. Four of us refused the price and made our way to a nearby small kiosk under the trees and refreshed ourselves with Pepsi Cola held in the usual buckets under ice blocks, while we allowed the driver to think his offer over. I was going to need some Indian Rupees from now on and so found the State Bank of India close by and exchanged a Travellers cheque. When I saw the date, 4th July, I wondered if Sue and Sandy had arrived in time for the full moon over the Taj.

We learned from the kiosk owner that there would shortly be a bus along and that the fare into town would be no more than one rupee each. As the time for the bus drew nearer the taxi driver's price began to lower until, as the dust of the bus was seen along the road a mile away, his price became a more reasonable 1.50R each. (16 Annas = 1 Paise; 100 Paise = 1 Rupee) We took the taxi.

Arriving in Amritsar, the talk of my fellow travellers was, 'Let's get to the Golden Temple'.

The Golden Temple actually meant nothing to me, for my preparation for the journey had been that of a long-distance runner rather than as a tourist with sites to visit. In the taxi with us from the border was a young French guy who wore the orange head gear of the Hari Krishna sect. He was going to the Temple to worship, and would I like to come along? We still had quite a few hours until the over-night train to Delhi and so, as an investigation of the spiritual life of the subcontinent, I said I would. A strange experience as we took off our sandals at the entrance.

The colonnaded outer part of the Hindu Golden Temple was in a poor state of neglect with peeling paint and plaster, and stonework that was becoming worn in being so open for centuries to the often-hostile elements. A small lake was in the middle and at the end of a short peninsula that reached out into the lake was the Golden Temple itself.

We queued with other faithful Hindus and slowly moved in line until we saw, under the dome, were sat several priests in orange robes and beards. With the murmurings from the priests, the people threw their offerings of money into large round trays. My friend was much enthused by the whole experience, his eyes growing wider with excitement as he practiced the chants, pulling at his thin beard as he stood in line. Bees were everywhere or were they wasps, as honey and sweetmeats seemed to also be part of the offering ritual.

Later we took a tuk-tuk taxi to the railway station and waited for the train to Delhi called the Frontier Mail. The

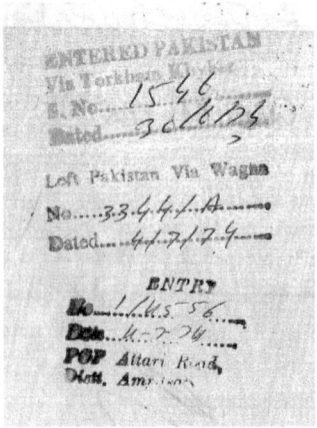

station was busy. We found a seat in a café to wait and took turns to get our tickets.

What we immediately noticed were a few hump-necked cows, brown and white, roaming aimlessly and endlessly, and that no one interfered with them even if they came too close. They were found in the waiting rooms, platforms and concourses and hallway ticket area where they defecated freely and without hindrance. Rather than move them out of the way, people moved themselves so as not to disturb them. My Hari Krishna friend told me the Hindu culture and tradition gives holy status to the cow and treats this sacred animal with reverence. Why? Because the cow is the highest giver of produce on earth; think milk, cheese, yoghurt and eventually meat, for human consumption yet leads a humble life.

There were also several dogs that roamed in groups around the area too, snatching what food they could. They were of no known western breed but, wolf-like and undomesticated, they also had the run of the place approaching seated people for food and scraps.

The station seemed the main place to find beggars, many with stunted or deformed bodies or missing limbs.

I was reminded of the story, probably apocryphal, of the benevolent low-caste father who took his baby to the railway line and allowed a train's wheels to sever a limb, knowing that in its life his child would always be able to beg for money rather than starve. One with birth deformities and only one limb with limited movement had a small, low trolley he scooted around on. Ingenious how some of the mobile platforms were adapted to individual disabilities. I had had summer jobs in Bristol's hospitals and knew that whatever your physical disability you were just given the large wheeled, two-handed, roll-it-yourself NHS wheelchair, that only an able-bodied person would have been able to move. Designed by an able-bodied person, of course.

Trying not to let the beggars catch your eye was a real skill as they came boldly up in their rags and poverty to beg for a few paise. My French friend insisted on giving alms to all and only attracted more to come to him. He looked at me with sideways glances to see if I was impressed and occasionally made his Hari Krishna chants.

Shortly before 7pm a station porter came up to try to persuade us to take a sleeper berth. We thought there was no real need for this. The station seemed pretty busy, yet not unreasonably so, and we took the decision that a night spent on a seat on the train would be fine. As long as we got on to the platform an hour, or at least 30 minutes before departure, we thought that would guarantee us a seat. The ticket office had a small glass window rather low down through which to ask for the ticket. There were at least 4 classes of travel, and we chose the basic 4th class. And as you read this, you are wondering if I had still learnt nothing from my Turkish rail experience.

More chai was needed in the heat, and we headed for the café where we decided to split the time difference and get to the platform 45 minutes before departure. Plenty of time we thought.

However, at our allotted time, the platform, so deserted an hour before, was now heaving with men and women with bags and luggage and children and commuters and army recruits, and so was the train, its windows and doors bursting with people. This was a shock to the system. As we arrived one soldier took up his metal trunk and, aiming it as a battering ram, ran at two men filling the doorway to a carriage, to get his place on the train. And these were the more expensive carriages.

We found a porter who directed us to the 4th class carriages. The first was full to overflowing, and we quickly moved along to the next and then the next. Finally, we had to do as others had done and force our way past the people blocking the doorway, and the people behind them, to gain entry. This compartment too was already full - beyond full. There was no seat available and only floor space enough to stand. After a long, exceptionally hot day we were now going to have to stand upright for the next 12 hours until we reached Delhi. Bodily contact with at least four other people was going to be an essential part of this trip, and their bodies were already hotter than ours and the air we were breathing had already been sucked into and vented out of at least fifty other pairs of lungs in the compartment.

The inside of my head was screaming. There was not even room to stretch a stiffening muscle, to bend the knee never mind sit on the floor. A wooden bench ran along the left side of the carriage in front of which sardined passengers sat on their luggage or stood hemmed-in, standing patiently in a Hindustani hypnotic trance. On the right were some partitioned compartments of seats but we could not see into them all. Baggage and children and men covered the luggage racks. They were the lucky ones.

I knew a nightmare of immense proportions was about to ensue. Squeezed so tight that it was impossible to get any water from my rucksack and with the temperature still of a high Indian summer night of over 100°F, I looked around over the sweating figures that were to be my travelling companions for the next half of a day and contemplated the end of my life.

I think it was on this journey, remembering how bad some of my travel experiences had been so far, that I played for the first time a mental game to keep me sane. It was simply called, 'If I had a gun, would I shoot myself now?' I would ask my tortured self this question over and over on this eleven-hour journey and the reply from my deepest self was always the same. My exhausted and febrile mind would shout the reply, heard by no-one but me. '*Yes! Give me the gun now!*'

A metal sign above a luggage rack noted for our benefit 'THIS COMPARTMENT TO CARRY 40 PERSONS ONLY'. I counted over 100 people, which included their floor bound luggage, estimating those that would be behind the partitions.

We never got to a seat. We stood at the same spot, a few feet from the door, unable to move for bodies and bags of all shapes and sizes. Next to me an elderly man, clothed only in a loin cloth, the length of which he draped over his shoulder, stood stoically and silently the whole of the journey. His head was bald except for the crown from which a circle of at least four feet of hair hung down his back. Later I understood he was a Jain who believed in the sacredness of all life and who would not even kill a mosquito or fly. At death they expected to be pulled immediately into paradise by their long hair.

The smell was of heat on human bodies, of dust and Indian spices. The open windows and doors wafted in the heated air of the Indian plains and that had only allowed my sweat and the dust of travel to collect and form another cardboard shirt. From 8pm on 4th July until 7am the next morning at Delhi station we had to stand. To this day, I don't know how I survived the journey; and how I envied the probably ticketless passengers who were risking their lives by riding on the outside of the train; yes, the OUT-SIDE of the train clinging to windows, door frames or were enjoying the breeze on the carriage roof. A few minutes into the journey I was past wondering what the Taj Mahal by moonlight might look like.

Chapter 13
Delhi

We drew up at Old Delhi station, fell off the train and gratefully took cups of chai from a station stall to restore some semblance of sanity and humanity. My French Hari Krishna follower was hungry and claimed he had no Indian money yet. He asked to borrow some to buy bananas and I had nothing smaller than a 10R note which he took. He then refused to give me the change. My reactions persuaded him to change his mind, and he quickly departed with his bananas but without my money. He was suddenly aware that something of his religious persona had slipped.

An Indian youth who looked like a university student had been in the same compartment and came up to me on the platform and offered to help me find a hotel. He wanted to try out his English having met a number of travellers like me before, and after a discussion he hailed a taxi for me and gave instructions to the driver.

The small hotel I was taken to was near Connaught Circus close to the centre of Delhi and was a large red brick building in the modern city just off the main wide boulevards. Several hippies and travellers were already staying there. I took a room and flaked out on the bed for the rest of the morning. Later, I had a shower and washed my clothes and then explored the area. I found a café. In the afternoon I hailed a Harley Davidson motorbike taxi driven by a burly Sikh and asked him to take me to the address at Gautam Nagar, which was the one Patrick Luby had given me at the Afghan border along with his small sketch map.

Gautam Nagar was a long, winding unpaved pathway that left the main road to the left of the large and sprawling compound that was the modern All-India Hospital. It was half a mile past a disparate collection of huts, workshops, stall holders and food street sellers that I saw three young white guys, stripped to the waist, working on the engine of a small truck. Twenty-five-year-old American Jay Sunanday was the leader of this group. He heard my story of travel and welcomed me with oily hands and a big smile. He told me to go inside and within a few minutes a bed in a shared room had been found for me.

This Christian organisation's base was a large bungalow, with a larger house behind which was the living quarters for the volunteer workers. These volunteers, mainly from churches in the USA, Britain and Europe, were the evangelists and/or mechanics who worked on repairing the vans and lorries that took the Word of God to all parts of the nation. You will remember that it had been to their HQ in Bombay that over the last year, working in Bristol, I had sent out the educational literature in the prison-made sacks.

The bungalow consisted of a small bookstore, office, and accommodation for the Delhi base's Indian manager Christopher, his wife, Rachel, and their two small children.

This organization and other Christian missionary groups were going through a difficult time, they told me. No more foreign missionaries were being allowed into India, and Christian Indians were being encouraged to take on any missionary organisation's leadership roles in their own country.

It was Christopher who explained to me the history of Christianity in India. It was not, as I had first thought, as a foreign import of the British Empire and its missionaries. There were credible traditional stories of Thomas and Bartholomew, both disciples of Jesus, bringing the gospel to Kerala and other parts of India in the first century, explained Christopher. When the Portuguese explorer Vasco da Gama arrived in Kerala on the south-west coast of India in 1498, he found Christians already here. When missionaries from Europe arrived in the eighteenth century they found a well-established Christian church in other parts of India too. The state of Kerala has a 20% Christian population. It appeared that it was a genuinely indigenous religion of India that was encouraged and benefited from foreign mission societies.

Jay was a wonderful Christian man whose heart was totally dedicated to his Lord and impressed me greatly by his humanity, humour and Christian witness to all; a born leader of men. I was deeply saddened later in the year when I was back in the UK to hear that he and two friends had all been killed when their car left the road in Yugoslavia when on their way back to the UK, overland.

Suppertime was when the team gathered and for 3 evenings a week the food would be western, and the other nights would be Indian. Brits were impressed by just how much meat we ate. Probably 3 or 4 times as much as we might eat in the UK; price is everything.

The first morning, I was asked to join a 150-metre-long queue for the bakers as there was a severe shortage of bread in the city and they would only give one loaf to each person in the queue, and we had a lot of mouths to feed.

I had told Jay about the bags I had sent to their Bombay office and meeting up with Patrick at the Afghan border. To my surprise he encouraged me, as I had time to spare, to travel on to Bombay to visit their HQ. This had never been a planned part of my trip. Touch Delhi and head home had been a plan somewhere. But the idea of seeing the destination of my post office mail bags was very tempting. So, on Thursday 11th July, I joined others from the base on our way to the railway station for the trip.

I left for Bombay by the Janata Express train at 8pm with Hugo from the Netherlands and an American called Tom. Tom was in a hurry. He needed to get to Sri Lanka to renew his visa for India before it ran out in five days. If he stayed in Shri Lanka a week he could then apply for another visa to come back to Delhi to continue his voluntary work.

This was to be another very uncomfortable journey through the night, but this time I was somewhat mentally prepared. The carriage was full when we arrived 15 minutes before departure. We could not force our way further in and so spent the first part of the journey sitting on the step of the carriage with the world passing by just feet away. Behind us people were sleeping on the luggage racks and sitting on luggage bundles on the floor as the benches were full. The journey was slow but the movement of air by the entrance this time, was some relief.

Express it was not. However, nor had the Erzurum Express lived up to expectations as it had travelled at no more than 30 or 40mph across Turkey; nor had the Frontier Mail been much faster. Nevertheless, with tonight's journey at 20 mph, even the Indian travellers were questioning the

NATIONAL AND GRINDLAYS BANK LIMITED
INCORPORATED IN THE UNITED KINGDOM
THE LIABILITY OF MEMBERS IS LIMITED

E-BLOCK, CONNAUGHT PLACE,
POST BOX NO. 13
NEW DELHI-110001.

TELEGRAMS GRINDLAY NEW DELHI
TELEPHONES: 43015, 43016, 44316, 43318, 47341

Date -8 JUL 1974

TO WHOM IT MAY CONCERN

We hereby certify that we purchased to-day foreign currency (as per details given below) from Mr. _____ (U.K.) holder of Pass Port No. A 536972 N dated 17-4-74 @ 17-4-54 and paid the net amount of Rs. 43/40 to him in lieu of Foreign Exchange so purchased.

Place N. Delhi
Date -8 JUL 1974

DETAILS OF Foreign Currency Purchased

Currency	Foreign or Currency i. e. travellers cheques currency notes Edt.	Amount
U.K.	Midland Bk T/c No. C/o - 289-549	£5

N.S. 96
REGISTERED IN ENGLAND: NO. 2945
REGISTERED ADDRESS: 23 FENCHURCH STREET, LONDON EC 3M 3BD

speed. Somewhere around 2am we arrived at Bharatpur Junction, a three-hour journey that had taken nearly 6 hours. We got off the train here, as Tom and Hugo had some church business to attend to. We hoped to try and get a faster train in the morning.

In the gloom of the night, we could see one platform at the end of which, standing dark and alone, was one small doorless waiting room. On examination it was empty except for a handful of homeless, tattered beggars and three or four small children resting on the dirt floor. Stray dogs with psychopathic eyes wandered continually in and out.

We barely slept and at about 7am we decided that we would walk into Bharatpur and find a bank, as Tom now revealed he had very little money. I said we could find a bank and change my Travellers cheques.

Tom and I set off for the town while Hugo did the church visiting. We walked for about a mile on a dirt track through some lush green forest with the sound of birds calling continually, until we came to a crossroads where a Pakistani tank with damaged tracks, captured during the recent war of 1972, was standing. Tom had told me we were in Rajasthan, the land of the Rajas, kings and rulers, with a proud military heritage.

A group of youths had gathered around the tank, and when they saw us we became an object of their curiosity. They hailed us and we called back a greeting. Then, probably because they suspected we were British from my accent, they started abusing us verbally.

'Bloody British. Why you not support Indians? Why you support Pakistan?'

The British government of the time had not taken India's side in their 1972 war with Pakistan, but nor had it sided with Pakistan. Britain's 'even-handed' approach to its allies and former colonies was to cost me dear before this trip was over. Then, the angry youths picked up stones and hurled them at us shouting something probably very impolite in their own language. We ran on!

The difference between the more rural towns and the cities was that here we were objects of curiosity and were stared at by most people who probably saw Europeans quite rarely. We were too early for the banks and found some chai to enjoy from a small shop as the town around us came to life and the day began to heat up.

Once they were open for business we entered each of the 'national' and 'international' banks, but none would change Travellers cheques. We walked up and down the main area of the town going in and out of banks with labels such as 'National Bank of India/ Rajasthan/ Gujarat' without any success, until eventually we came to the Punjab National Bank. Would it cash Travellers cheques? Probably not. We were wrong.

We were ushered upstairs and there, under a cooling fan, they went through the documentation, typed it all up, and gave us 69R for my £4.00 Travellers cheques. (£4.00 in 1974 would equate in Britain to about £80.00 in 2023, believe it or not!)

Back at the station the three of us bought our tickets to travel on to Bombay. We managed to book sleepers for the journey which took us from Friday at 4pm until Saturday night at 11pm.

Metal trunks for travel were as much a feature here in this rural station as in the cities. Nobody bothered with leather that would mould and decay in the heat and humidity. Families could sit on a metal trunk; put a baby to sleep on them; share lunch on them, play games on them and barge your way into a crowded carriage with them. And if there was no room on a bench to sit - then it was your journey's rest.

The monsoons had started as we soon discovered the nearer we travelled to Bombay. In the fields a large black umbrella, as if from a London gentleman's outfitters, shielded a man as he worked his plot of land, while others we passed gathered under trees or walked with huge green leaves over their heads until a rain shower had passed.

As the train pulled into each of the innumerable stations, eager eyes peered into the carriages and sellers of food and drink would pile onboard. Ragged beggars also invaded the carriages swiftly moving their deformed bodies through, begging for alms as they offered to show us their deformities.

Again, I was warned that to give to one would be to invite a crowd of them, and so we avoided eye contact as much as we could. They were also at the open yet barred windows as well, imploring you to make eye contact and extract sympathy and money to live.

After a long viaduct high over a wide river and flood plain we stopped at another station. A young man came to the window begging and trying to charm us by smiling and trying out some English. Tom saw him eyeing up my Seiko watch and warned me to put my arm away before the man

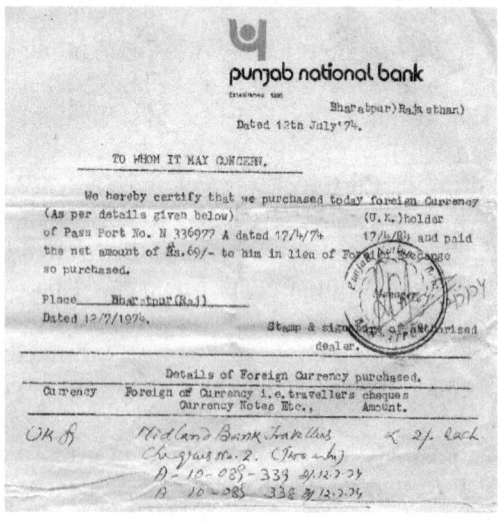

could snatch at it as the train pulled out.

The wooden fold-down bench for the night was hard and unforgiving to my body that had now lost much of its excess flesh in my month of travels. But the memory of a previous night of travel on Indian Railways left me very grateful for these simple planks of wood. As we approached Bombay we could see the flooding of the fields and roads and the disruption caused by the monsoon. What state would the city be in?

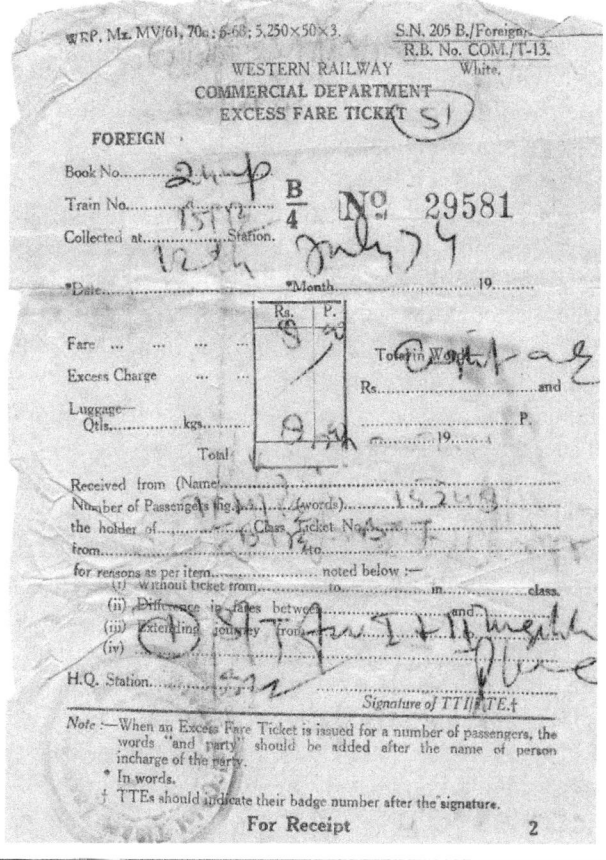

Chapter 14
Bombay/Mumbai

The monsoons had struck Bombay a week earlier and the city, lying as it does on a peninsular surrounded on three sides by the sea and being very low-lying, the rainwater always had difficulty draining away. If it rained for more than two hours the sewers regularly flooded and could flood into the clean water system. Flooding had also shut down the city's electric and diesel trains; motor vehicles had found key roads impassable and the only transport that usually could still get about was the old horse-drawn cabs. Late at night and with the city's roads now beginning to clear of water we managed to find a motor taxi to take us to the offices in Worli Road.

As we neared Bombay my curiosity about the mail bags increased. Would I find the post bags there? For me now, Bombay was journey's end; the end of my hippie trail journey, although not the whole adventure as I still had the return journey to navigate. I only had to get back to Istanbul, and travel and food through India, Pakistan, Afghanistan and Turkey was extremely cheap. I had enough rupees and cheques to see me through India anyway and Magic Bus in Istanbul would then whisk me back to London. I had collected money in each of the countries I had travelled through and would be happy to unload them on the trip home. The only fly in the ointment was whether I had enough money to get through Afghanistan; $100US or equivalent was what I would need to get through there again.

We were up on the second floor of the concrete building in Worli Road. There were a number of offices, and the seven Indian workers and three or four western volunteers slept on the floor in the various rooms. I found a comfortable place under a desk, and this was no discomfort compared with the beds I had slept in during my six weeks of travelling.

In the morning the cook came into the kitchen and, pulling at her yellow and pink rose-petal sari sleeve, took up the cooking pot and poured in the contents of the bag of sugar she had bought at the local shop. She was dark and so from south India and a gold stud rested in the hollow of her nose. She poured boiled water from a jug into the saucepan just enough to cover the sugar. Then she took a spoon and took out the tiny, black bugs that had floated to the top. Finally, she boiled the sugar water and let it cool and the sugar re-crystallise. Now it was edible.

That Sunday morning, we breakfasted on fruit, bread and coffee. Outside, we saw the first things one had to get used to in Bombay. That the pavements of the side streets were not for walking on; you walked in the road. On looking out of the window on my first morning, the local people from the apartment blocks close by, were squatting for all to see to do their morning ablutions. Piles of poo from men, women and children littered the pavements. I was told that over 100,000 people slept on the streets of Bombay every night.

I joined the workers and volunteers as we all travelled to a Pentecostal church by crowded Bombay bus. It was a 20-minute ride away - but there were few stares of curiosity in this city even though the Christian workers were the only Europeans who travelled regularly by bus. At the church I was introduced to Ray who was the mission chief in India, and he invited Tom and myself back for lunch to his flat to the north of Bombay in the village of Versova.

Two long bus rides awaited us; the first of about 40 minutes to get to the northern limits of the city, a place called Enderi. The bus was jam-packed, and I stood with one hand gripping the bar above me on the lower deck of the very British double decker. Above me was a sign that read, 'Only 40 standing passengers allowed'. There were so many more, and no-one was counting, but I remembered the Bristol buses had a similar sign that read, 'Only 5 standing passengers allowed'.

The roads were crowded with more overladen lorries with colourful decoration, cars, bicycles, motorbikes and smaller motorcycles and tuk-tuk taxis; animal-drawn vehicles of all sizes, and men carrying loads on their backs or pulling or pushing carts. And cows - the ubiquitous cows - moving in front of us and across the roads halting traffic. The sit-up-and-beg black bicycles were sometimes so loaded with goods there was no place left for the cyclist to sit, so it was pushed.

The Morris Oxford car was everywhere with metal sun-visors. This vehicle had long ago been left behind in 50s Britain when the factory had moved out here. This was the vehicle of choice for so many, looking quite incongruous now so far from its cultural home. Sunday of course, was just another working day for the other religious groups and so the traffic was as heavy as any weekday and the temperature and humidity very high.

Over lunch with Ray and his East German wife Christa, he told us his story. Ray had been adopted by American missionaries in India because his Indian mother had rejected him at birth. As a result, he could claim both Indian and US citizenship and so was able to continue his missionary work uninterrupted by any new government rules about foreign workers. Ray and Christa had adopted two Indian babies, now toddlers.

Water in their flat was held in buckets and bowls, everywhere, even in the bathroom to flush the toilet. In the evening local people came to the beach to do their own toilet quite openly. It was said that the beaches in Bombay were the only toilets in India that flushed twice a day!

Returning to the offices in Worli Road the next day, Monday, I climbed the stairs and on entering, I heard someone shout, 'The mail has come.'

Inside the front door stood a large, brown sack of mail. Could this be one of the mail sacks that I had packed up months ago when I was working in Bristol? It looked very familiar. The labels looked right too. I flipped the label over and on the back of this large British post office bag was my own handwriting giving the weight and my signature. Is life simply just a random jumble of events and incidents?

The Worli road offices were by no means a male preserve. The female workers lived in a flat down near the docks and joined us by minibus for the working day and evening meal. Personal relationships between male and female volunteers or employees were discouraged in order to present a high moral standard in this conservative country.

The offices were somewhat cramped, and most spaces were taken up with some form of Christian literature storage or work. In my first week I spent the days sorting books but the very high temperature and high humidity, a damp wet heat, was very oppressive even for the Indians, for there were no fans or air-conditioning.

The sun was not to be seen because of the humidity but we felt its effects! It made working difficult for the energy was soon sapped out of you each day. A German volunteer, Heinrich, had flown out from Germany that week to spend two years volunteering with them. He found the heat extraordinarily oppressive, and one could see him each day struggling to cope and focus on his tasks. Within a fortnight he was advised to leave and return to Europe, which he gratefully did.

I had met Pip and Tony, who had also joined us for lunch that Sunday with Ray and Christa, and they invited me to supper later in the week. They asked what I would like to eat. Jokingly, I said, 'Anything English, how about fish and chips'.

From their kind and generous hearts that is what they served a few nights later. It was the greatest meal I had had after all that my stomach had had to put up with over the last month of indiscernible-meat-with-potatoes or rice, and vegetable soups and flat bread! Yellow chips and fish-in-batter cooked to crispy perfection in their flat in a high-rise block in downtown Bombay; wonderful!

Tony was bearded even in this heat and Pip was beautiful and slim in her long flowing dress and covered shoulders. Their flat overlooked an apartment block next door, and we could look down onto the rooftop where a family was eating and the children playing tag in the evening heat.

It was that evening with Tony and Pip that I met Brian who was the chief mechanic for the organisation and its transport services and who was based in Calcutta. He was in his late 40s and as he was British he had no visa troubles in India. However, his presence in India was considered by some, 'undesirable', and the Calcutta police were anxious to have him deported.

The Indian police chief in Calcutta was an Indian Christian but was against the idea of volunteer workers coming in from abroad. He had good reasons for this. His argument was that if Christian western volunteers were able to go to India and work and evangelise, then other more politically motivated groups might be allowed the same privileges. The communists particularly were actively engaged in terrorist and subversive activities in the eastern States which the Indian government was struggling to suppress.

A Brit called Mike came to stay at Worli road for a few days. He had been working in Iran and had come across to see something of India. In the evenings, the workers were in the habit of going into a local Indian café for supper and on this occasion it was Mike, myself and a Brit called David.

I made it a habit to choose carefully from the menu on the advice of my new friends. For unless you said very, very clearly that you didn't want any chilies in any of your food from omelette to soup or bread etc, the cook would put plenty in and it would be almost too hot to eat.

The waiter came over to serve us and we ordered drinks and bowls of food, with a strict instruction of 'no chilis please', but with plenty of chapatis to go with it. When it came the food was still hot in both senses for it seemed incomprehensible to street café cooks that anyone would not want chilies in their food. We picked out the offending items. I was assured by David that the water in the café was safe to drink, but then I made a mistake that I would sincerely regret.

My mistake was that when asked if I wanted ice in my water I said, yes. The thought that this was a gamble of whether the ice was from the same safe source as the water or just from the tap didn't occur to me. It should have, bearing in mind the recent flooding of the clean water system in the monsoon. Almost before the meal was over the contents of my stomach was searching for a quick exit. My companions seemed unaffected. They had not had ice.

It was not until the next day that I was sick and everything in my stomach had been emptied down the hole-in-the-floor toilet. I was drained of energy and over the next few days became weakened and dehydrated. I went without food to try to starve the bug, as some advised. Others thought eating bananas would seal you up. Others bought some kind of herbs for me in a packet from a local store. However, through that week no matter what little I ate or drank I stayed very sick and for three of those days I went without food completely.

Ray saw my condition and invited me to stay with him and his family at Versova. I did, but by the following Tuesday Christa suggested I go to the doctor in Enderi.

The doctor gave me an injection, some tablets to take and told me I had some kind of 'gastro-enteritis'. He then handed me a bottle of some brown liquid with a good deal of sediment in the bottom. A couple of days later and for another 10R he gave me another injection. After leaving his surgery I found myself seeking the back of a building and coughing my guts up.

Ray, that gracious man, came to collect me from the bus stop and we walked back to his flat through the dark lanes. He suggested I go to the German hospital in Bombay tomorrow for treatment. Ray and Christa were such a lovely, gracious couple and generous to a fault in their kindness towards me.

In their lounge Christa and Ray had a poster, a quotation from the Bible from the book of Habakkuk.

> *'Though the fig trees do not blossom.*
> *and there is no fruit on the vine,*
> *though the olive crops fail*
> *and the fields lie barren,*
> *the sheep die in the folds.*
> *and the cattle stalls are empty,*
> *yet I will rejoice in the Lord,*
> *I will glory in the God of my salvation.'*

That was going to be a challenge to me.

What was to be the end of this drama of sickness? I was still so far from home and depending on the generosity of others. I was about to go into hospital. These hospital bills will be impossible to pay. How on earth could I travel back to the UK overland in this sick state, as I could not afford the plane fare? Some form of miracle was needed.

My starved and aching body returned to Worli road by bus the next day, Friday. In the afternoon I went with one of the Indian workers to the German hospital about half a mile away. Yet even walking there in the heat was a huge strain. But at least they could get my body back to health, I thought. But what a shock. The hospital gates were locked; lights were off. What? Why?

Enquiries were made of the caretaker behind the barred gate. His explanation was quite reasonable – to him. It was Friday 2nd August and a Parsi holiday. By tradition the members of that religion would go to the beach on this day and throw coconuts into the sea hoping for good things in the coming year.

Parsis, I later learned, are a religious group in India of Iranian prophet Zoroaster, a prophet of seventh century B.C.. Originally from greater Iran, they migrated to India to avoid persecution by Muslims. The Parsi population is mainly concentrated in Mumbai and towns to the north of the city along the Gujarat border.

The hospital closure was the most dreadful news. How on earth could this be happening to me? I staggered back to Worli road confused and confounded. All my efforts of going to the medical doctor and now the hospital for healing had failed. The hospital was now closed over the weekend, and I would have to wait until Monday, a lifetime away, to get help. A deep depression set in.

That Saturday, I took a shower and saw in a mirror my emaciated state. I was 14 stone when I left the UK and had always had some padding around my middle. I had never seen the outline of my ribs or my hips in my entire life until - that is - I looked in this mirror. The last of the medicine made me sick again and the tablet came up immediately it was swallowed with what looked like blood. Could I be in such a darker place, I thought, as I drifted to sleep that Saturday night in my bed on the floor under the desk?

At 6am for the last week or more I had been sick on waking, but this Sunday I was not. As the morning wore on and no sickness came my way I began to walk around the offices wondering that my state today was not quite the same as it had been in the previous ten days. I hesitantly began to wonder if I was over the worst of it. One of the Indian brothers offered me a large, green pear to eat. I put it to one side and thanked him.

After lunch, which I didn't have, I still felt 'unsick'. My spirits began to rise - just a little. Could I dare to try to eat that pear? It was *so* tempting to my food deprived body. It was huge and fresh, green and soft to the touch, ripe and so appealing. A quiet confidence was growing in me that the worst was over. Yes, I was unwell, but not being sick, I was thin and probably dehydrated for my stomach even refused chlorinated water.

Early in the afternoon my confidence was such and the appeal of the large pear so great that I took a bite, chewed and swallowed. My stomach lurched a bit. It wasn't used to food. I waited. I didn't feel I was to be sick. I ate some more of the pear and the juice trickled off my chin. Within an hour, bite by bite I had consumed it with no ill effects at one end or the other. I rejoiced.

In my 'knower' I now knew I was over it. I was over it! Was this a miracle! It was definitely a miracle of timing!

Chapter 15
The Return

The following Tuesday 13th, much recovered in body and spirit, I was at the Victorian edifice which was the Bombay Railway station, where flocks of pigeons and all varieties of beggars had made their home. I left by the 6am train to Delhi, arriving mid-afternoon the following day to stay again at Gautam Nagar. My sweet tooth was now demanding feeding. I found a store and bought a bar of Indian chocolate and broke it in half. It was full of holes, but not the Aero kind. I tapped it like one of Nelson's crew might have tapped the ship's biscuit expecting a weevil to come out. None did. I ate it - quickly.

From my sickbed in Bombay, this was the return plan I had worked out and Delhi was to be my first stop on my way back to the UK.

By Sunday 1st September I needed to be in Istanbul to catch the Magic Bus back to the UK that morning. Working backwards, I would need time for a two-day train ride across from Erzurum which meant I had to leave that city in eastern Turkey by Thursday night 29th August, to arrive in Istanbul by the Saturday. I should therefore try to be in Tehran by Tuesday the 27th August and to leave that day by coach to make sure I got to Erzerum a day early, i.e., Wednesday night. If I could catch Wednesday's train to Istanbul that would be better than Thursday night's train if possible.

From Delhi that gave me ten days to get across Pakistan and Afghanistan and on to Tehran. Now I had to make a choice. Would cutting out Afghanistan make the journey shorter? Frankly, I didn't think I could do that desert journey again nonstop. Would the route south through Pakistan to Iran be much simpler? Anyway, there was another problem of making sure I had £15GB for entry into Afghanistan. I know that doesn't seem much money now, but then it was a nice bundle to use in a low-cost world like Afghanistan. I had money in many currencies. I knew money was waiting for me in a Tehran bank, sent by my brother. But that was the other side of Afghanistan.

Thursday 15th August was the National Independence Day holiday and Indira Gandhi, India's prime minister, had celebrated it early at 7am at the Red Fort, before the heat set in.

The newspaper *The Times of India* was then a thin newssheet compared to any London paper, and allegations it published against Mrs. Indira Gandhi, almost daily, of corruption would have brought down any UK Prime Minister. Most of the news was of course about India and it was hard to find any information about the UK within its pages. Something did catch my eye about Turkey invading Cyprus

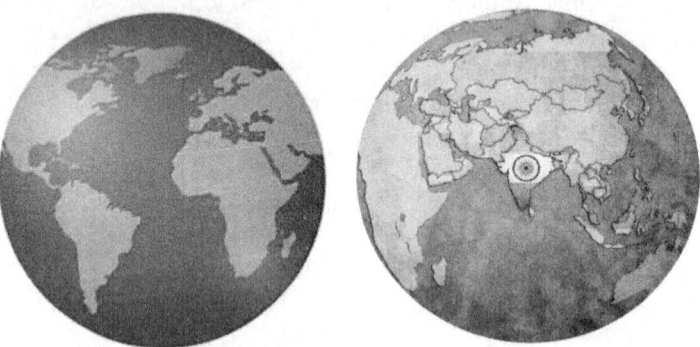

but that was of no interest to me.

In those days I had been a regular reader of *Newsweek* and *Time* magazines. At the top of the front page of *Time* there always appeared a picture of the world globe. Seeing the Indian edition of *Time* in the shops in Delhi, for a moment I was confused. I didn't recognize our world. What planet was this?

The so familiar world map had the Americas on the left separated from Europe and Africa by the wide Atlantic Ocean, with the UK prominent in the high centre. In the UK editions there was no India or Asia or Australia or the Pacific islands.

Now, here on the Indian magazine cover was a world I struggled to recognize. No Americas or the bulge of Africa; I looked again. India with Asia was now central, and Africa and Europe squeezed to the left with Britain a tiny dot of an offshore island close to the North Pole. Britain was insignificant. The Americas were lost to view. How could the United States of America, and Great Britain, both so influential in world affairs simply be lost to view?

More than anything in my travels this brought home to me the very narrow ideas I had of the world up to that time. My Anglo-centric view was too parochial and maybe the world's superpower, the USA, while important to Europe, was really not a power player in this part of Asia. How times would change.

Friday I visited the Chartered Bank in Delhi where my family had sent me some money. Behind the open desk sat a large Muslim gentleman with a deep, black moustache who opened a large register and thumbed through its thick volume looking at the money payment orders that had come to them over the last month. Behind him in this large building as far as the eye could see, clerks dressed in white shirts with bits of paper in their hands moved from section to section or desk to desk enabling business and personal banking to progress in the city. This was life in a busy Indian bank in the last decade before the advent of computers.

He had bad news, and he gave it to me straight. 'Very sorry, the money has not come into our bank. Are you sure this is the right bank. There are many banks, you know.'

'Then where could it be?' I asked confused. I needed to start my homeward journey a.s.a.p. and didn't want any further delay.

He was a little stoney-faced, I think not wanting criticism of his employer. 'Somewhere in England, Europe or any country in between, or another bank. But not here,' was his unsmiling, dismissive reply.

I left feeling a touch angry and frustrated. This was useful money for my return trip. However, banks are open in India on Saturdays, and something made me determined to visit the bank again the next day.

I made my way the six miles into Delhi on a motor bike taxi, walked into the bank and up to the same man at the same desk and boldly said to him, 'I have come to collect my money.'

He didn't bat an eyelid but raised them instead. 'Ah, we are terribly sorry. We found your money after you left yesterday. It had been put into a different file. We are very sorry.'

A wave of relief swept over me. With the paperwork done, he gave me the cheque which I cashed at his bank.

Feeling a millionaire with 300R in my pocket I went immediately to the American Express office and changed most of them into US dollars, as I had learnt the hard way that this was the best currency for international travel. I remember treating myself to an ice-cool drink and ice cream at an open-air café, and later had the experience of another encounter with an Anglo-Indian student who wanted to ask me all about England.

I had read and heard about Connaught Circus in the centre of Delhi as having the largest café in India, or South-east Asia or the world; the All-India Café. Some library book I had thumbed through before I came on this trip also described it as the end of the hippy trail; i.e., the centre of the capital city.

On my way I was about to cross the street in Old Delhi when I saw, lying sprawled across a traffic island, his head and shoulders in the road and his legs upon the kerb, a young boy of about twelve years of age – clearly dead. I studied him for more than a moment. No movement, no breathing and flies hovered uninterrupted about his mouth. I had no idea of the cause of death. A traffic accident perhaps.

Pedestrians seemed unconcerned and simply stepped over his body to go on their way. Was this the normal way of life and death in India? India's population then was a staggering 520 million (now it is over one billion) and I guessed about ten million of those would die every year. I was bothered by my own response. What should I do? What could I do? Whose child was this? What mother was anxiously missing her child?

The All-India Café was a huge dome of a place with multiple entrances around its circular edge. Always crowded with tables large and small and with very large numbers of Indian men with small moustaches standing by, keen and eager to serve you. But it was here, also, that you met the wreckage of the hippie trail, the lives that had been ruined by drugs indulged so cheaply along the way.

As I sat down I found a tall, lean American pulling up the chair next to me.

'Can you buy me some chai?' he pleaded without making eye contact. 'I don't have any money on me at the moment.'

The waiter caught my eye, and I ordered drink and food for us both. His story was one that I would find each time I came here over the next few days and all the men seemed to be lean and gaunt and from the USA.

The story for each was that they had 'lost' their passport. They had informed the US Embassy who were organizing a new one. Yes, family back home was sending them money to live on, and when the new passport came through they would be sent money to buy an air ticket home. It could all seem very plausible.

But, in fact, the 'lost' passport had probably been sold for drugs, informed sources told me later. It was true that the US Embassy did renew passports - but only once. The rumour was that a number of these men at the Café had sold their second passports too and cashed in the money for the air ticket sent from home. The money would have been spent on drugs and they were now stuck in India with no hope of another passport. i.e., stateless and homeless. Unless the family continued to send them money, they could simply beg or starve. The All-India Café was almost a guarantee that they would meet some touring westerners to whom they could attach themselves and tell their tale.

I had heard about a house in a New Delhi suburb that was run by a Christian group trying to rehabilitate former western drug users. My Christian friends were keen to show me before I left. Still recognisable as hippies by their clothes and beards, they were a cheerful group of 5 residents, far enough away from temptation in the city in this anonymous square mile of bungalows, a 20-minute motor-cycle taxi ride from the city centre.

They had fought their addiction with a mixture of prayer, cold-turkey and a newfound Christian faith. If these former hippies had ever sought an authentic eastern religion experience at the end of their travels, they had found it. Jesus was middle eastern and his church in India had a long history of authenticity. His disciples had just to follow the Red Sea from Israel down to the Arabian Gulf, and Hindustan was off to the left. Here, these guys looked clean and could look you in the eye as they talked. They sounded like people freed from a form of slavery who were now seeing a colourful world through new eyes, as they told of the desperate life they had been living under the curse of drug addiction. You had to admire their courage and determination.

Back at Gautam Nagar that evening I was introduced to an Indian Christian for whom you could only have enormous respect. He was of a great age, bespeckled with long white hair and beard and his name was Brother Jacob. His only possession was a black sit-up-and-beg bicycle and his dhoti around his waist. He was very well known amongst Christian churches and groups as he had travelled endlessly for so many years as an evangelist from the northern-most parts of Kashmir to the southernmost regions of India.

Brother Jacob's story was heartbreaking. As a young man he had been the headmaster of a Christian school. In 1933 his wife and their three daughters had died in an epidemic. He gave up his job and decided to travel all over the country into every State on his bicycle preaching the gospel and lived by faith in all that time.

Brother Jacob's was a life of gentleness and kindness to everyone as he preached the love of Jesus to all who would listen. Passing through towns he would stay with churches or missionary groups and aid them in their work.

Chapter 16
Lahore to Quetta

Now it was time to begin the journey back to the UK, and when it came to my departure from Gautam Nagar, Brother Jacob walked with me the half mile to the taxi rank and saw me off. He had wanted to come to the station to see me on the train. I persuaded him not to and I thanked him for his kindness in coming so far. His humility, warmth and compassion left a great impression on me.

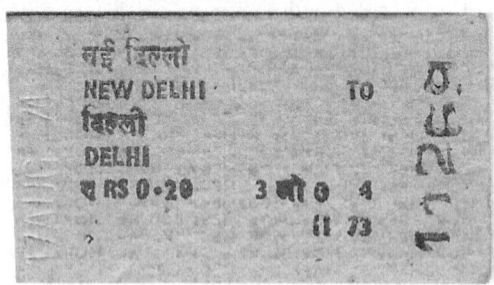

I paid the 1.50R motorcycle taxi to New Delhi railway station and caught the commuter train to the Old Delhi station.

Here in the evening, I caught the 9.30pm Frontier Mail train and this time I bought myself a sleeping berth.

We travelled through the night, arriving in Amritsar early, about 6am on Tuesday 20th August. I took the local bus straight away to the Wagha border for 60 paise.

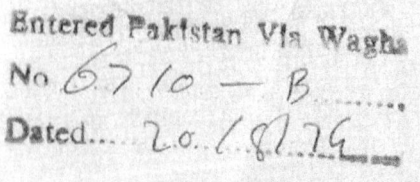

Passing through the border later that morning I met two English girls with rucksacks who were on their way back to the British Embassy in Pakistan where their parents worked. They had had a few weeks exploring India and experiencing the full moon at the Taj Mahal. Clean, fresh, confident, beautiful, articulate, middle-class English girls from a public school somewhere in the home counties, I guessed, who would never have included themselves as being on any part of the hippie trail.

I had hoped to get my Parker pen back from the official I had met here 8 weeks previously. Sadly, he was not to be seen.

Once across the border I took the bus to Lahore hoping to see Sidney Igguldon at the vicarage. He was not there. I left a message and returned to the station to catch the 2pm train south to Quetta. Yes, I had decided against travel through Afghanistan this time.

Despite the collection of money in my pocket, I had become uncertain if I had enough money to enter Afghanistan. One hundred US dollars or £15GB or equivalent was needed, and I had seen how the Afghan officials did make checks at the border. But nor did I want the long sweltering journey by bus from Lahore up to the Khyber Pass border and then risk being refused entry. If I was not able to travel through the country then my small collection of Afghanis was useless. Also, I began to realise that I would do anything to avoid the Khyber Pass to Kabul to Kandahar to Herat post bus three or four-day journey again.

Hence I decided to travel the rail route down through the south-western part of Pakistan through Quetta and on to Taftan on the Iranian border. I had met a guy at the All-India Café who had talked about this route. The same route as the two hippies who had refused to have their hair cut on the Iran/Afghan border back in June. It too was desert, still safe to travel but the train would be easier than the many days spent on the oven like buses.

I was at the Lahore station platform early; experience had taught me this! A few people were seated in the carriages as I found a place on the slatted wooden benches. There were no compartments, just rows of benches along either side facing the front. I decided against a sleeper. I would be fine as I now had a seat, and I needed to save money anyway. The windows were simply barred to let in the air, and this was another 'express' train for which 40mph was to be its speed limit, as it made its leisurely way across the dry, flat and desert landscape of Pakistan. As we travelled through small towns and remote villages the train began to fill up.

A Pakistani family, of Dad in shirt and slacks and Mum in her beautifully flowered shalwar-chemise with a boy of about seven years-old joined us and sat on the hard benches across the aisle from me. We exchanged glances and smiles, and as the day wore on they took out their basket of food for the journey. They later offered me some of their chapatis and fruit. It was a kind offer, but the heat always took away my appetite. I declined with a grateful smile, a shake of my head and put the hand across my chest but made many thanks. It was the Muslim culture of hospitality that was expressed to me for which I was very grateful.

Early afternoon we stopped at a nameless station and the family departed with smiles and waves.

The train restarted and I made my way to the restaurant car. Again, I found myself the object of great curiosity from the 30 or so men of all ages, as the only European on the train. No women were in the restaurant car. I took chai and quietly stared back. There was no hostility from them. Just curiosity. What were their thoughts?

Throughout my Asian trip I had found myself the object of curiosity by many people, and they would think nothing of just staring at me silently and at whatever I was doing. On this occasion only by meeting their gaze did they, after a few minutes, decide to move their eyes away and pretend to give their attention to something else; until I too looked away and they could stare again.

Years later I had the same experience in visiting our daughter when she was teaching in South Korea. On a Bullet Train ride from Seoul to Ulsan an older Korean woman simply stood up in the carriage and stared at us for two hours on the journey; expressionless, but intensely curious about everything we did.

As the Pakistan night drew on, there was enough room for me to lie down. Nevertheless, I knew that the wooden benches were going to be somewhat punishing to my now boney frame.

The following morning, another stop and looking out of the window I saw a vendor selling hot food from a stall on the platform of this small station. My hunger had finally got the better of me and I knew I should eat something before arrival at Quetta. I dismounted as people were milling around and the train showed no sign of building up steam and moving off again.

I pointed to something on the stall to fill a chapati and, as the vendor prepared the food, Pakistani men on the platform turned around and began to stare at me. Just to stare, expressionless. My guess was that this had happened to Europeans from their first setting foot in the country centuries ago. My great grandfather had served in the British army in India from about 1857 to 1890 and my grandmother had been born there in Gwalior along with her many brothers. Was I experiencing what they had experienced? The stranger in the midst, the outsider. I took no offence, and none attempted to speak to me.

On the opposite platform two soldiers in khaki uniforms held hands and laughed and joked together, which puzzled me somewhat. Then the food was ready, money exchanged, and I took one bite. Wowzer! It was extremely hot and, as I did my best to control any facial expression of horror, I nonchalantly turned away from the onlookers and walked back to the train and, climbing aboard, immediately spat out the offending food through the window on the other side. Had I said, 'No chilies, thank you,'? I hadn't.

By the time the train arrived in the sand-coloured township of Quetta on Wednesday 21st in the afternoon, I was feeling quite exhausted and somewhat depressed. What with the heat, lack of sleep again and lack of travelling companion a sense of loneliness had set in.

Quetta was quite unlike towns on the hippie trail. Of course, I was off the trail now in southern Pakistan and I was to be here only for a few hours. None of the facilities associated with the hippie trail were evident; no cafés, or cheap hotels and no hippies either. I asked at the station for the next train to the border with Iran.

'*Saturday,*' was the reply. Some consternation! I did not want to hang around for 3 days in this desert town. They also told me no buses went to the border. Surely not!

I found a small café and asked the owner for a hotel. They spoke enough English to indicate they didn't know of one but offered me a back room with an earthen floor to rest in. I think they could see that the heat had so sapped the energy out of me. I slept gratefully for an hour, and then thanked them profusely.

There followed a great deal of walking around and asking people who I hoped spoke English. Late afternoon I did find a bus company's offices. Yes, they did go to the border with Iran. The cost of a coach to the border with the Super Fine Tourist Service was 35 Rupees. I bought the ticket with a high expectation of comfort from this company's name. A better journey surely than the Saidkhan Taransport Bus to Kabul. I had to be at the bus station at 6am the next day. At this point I had still not been able to find a hotel to stay for the night.

But close by I did find a small guest house of mud bricks and glassless, shuttered windows. I was shown to a small windowless back room. The walls were unformed mud bricks, the floor of earth, the bed a rough wooden frame with rope across it on which to lie; the same kind of rope bed I had experienced in Lahore and probably the best bed to lie on in the heat; rough planks of frayed wood made up the unlockable door to the alleyway.

It was to be an early night for sleep. Disturbed by some mosquitoes, I slept intermittently until about 4am.

Chapter 17
Quetta to the Iran Border

That morning, early, I was at the Super Fine Tourist Service offices and met the only other European travelling with me. He was Italian and about my age with a thin small beard. He didn't speak English and I didn't speak Italian, so he called me John and I called him Peter.

My disappointment with the transport was great but you are probably well ahead of me on this too. The vehicle was no 'Super Fine' anything. It was the same kind of snub-nosed, metal box post bus I had travelled on from Herat to Kabul! Why did I think it could have been anything else?

Goats and chickens were already being loaded onto the roof rack with all manner of turbaned and baggy-trousered men and children and large baggage. This journey from Quetta to the border was 600 kilometers and would last until the afternoon of the next day which would be the Friday evening. I didn't want to think too much about it.

At 6am that Thursday morning, the oppressive heat felt over 100°F already. The bus was packed with many Baluchi tribespeople, some of the men again with what looked like British Lee-Enfield .303 rifles on their shoulders and bandoleers of bullets across their chests. I wondered if some poor British soldier had given his life in the service of one of his country's failed foreign policies for this Baluchi to display it now.

The Lee-Enfield .303 rifle had been the standard weapon for British and colonial forces, including in the area we know today as India, Pakistan, and Afghanistan during the first half of the 20th Century. It would also have been used by the UK military in its deployment of troops in Iran and Iraq in the 1920s and 30s. I had proved myself a marksman with it on the rifle range in 1965 as a Corporal in the school's Army Cadet Force.

If they were unsmiling, no one was unfriendly as I found my way inside climbing over the statutory huge bales of corn to a hard bench by a window. For most of the journey Peter travelled on the roof of the bus, a makeshift turban wrapped around his head as protection from the sun. He had the benefit of a bronzed Mediterranean colouring to my English freckles and white skin. To my relief the bus was on a good, smooth tarmac road.

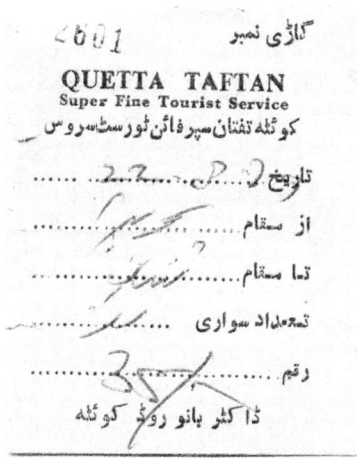

Fourteen hours later, after regular stops for obligatory prayers by the Baluchis on board and some small villages where refreshments could be found, we eventually reached the point where the tarmac ran out and the dirt road began. No warning - and without slowing we hit the dirt road and suddenly every part of the bus, which had neither suspensions nor shock absorbers, was vibrating, rattling and shaking.

Through the windshield of dirt in the evening's dying

light, I could see the desert road ahead now ridged, furrowed and grooved with random black holes for the driver to avoid – if he chose. Behind, we were throwing up a grey dust cloud. With no cushioning suspensions, every ridge and hole were experienced. But the stoic passengers around me gripped the back of the seat in front of them and just stared out of the front window at the road ahead, silent, impassive, resigned, transfixed.

Sleep of any kind was now out of the question as we were hitting the ridges at two a second and the noise inside the bus and my head was like that of a pneumatic drill.

Each hamlet, village or community we passed was separated by hours of travel and as we drove through, each was indistinguishable from another. Dark, mud brick houses of a single story and a flat roof, but one of the mud buildings always had a dome which presumably was the mosque. I wondered at the skill of creating a dome from mud.

About 1am the bus slowed and stopped at what appeared to be, in the darkness, another small hamlet. However, this proved to be a long meal stop to refresh the driver and passengers. We crawled over the wheat sacks to get our feet on solid ground, appreciating the sudden silence and loss of vibration.

In the cool of the Pakistan night, Peter and I chose some rice and meat and chai to drink from the large, shallow pans held over smouldering cinders in front of a stall outside a darkened building. We sat with the other travellers in a large circle around a glowing brazier. Around us our fellow travellers, Afghan, Pakistani or Iranian ate and drank too and talked in hushed tones, some still in possession of their firearms, beneath a bare, black sky full of starlight.

The thought occurred to me that if any of them assumed we were rich westerners carrying much money, they could rob us, kill us and bury us in the sand. No one would ever know what became of us. But they were all faultlessly polite, even if they largely ignored us. I was aware, not for the first time on this journey, that we were probably living in parallel worlds; our life experiences and values allowed us to remain separate even though we were having the same physical experiences. We were just interpreting the events of our lives differently.

Strengthened by the break and the food and drink we continued our way and, with the continual hammering from the road, sleep and rest were again forsaken. As the punishing nightmare progressed, into my mind crept that self-murder game; 'If I had a gun, would I shoot myself now?' 'Yes! Yes! Yes!' Every time the answer was, 'Yes! Gimme the gun now!'

The heat had gone from the day and the desert night and Peter was now inside the bus, afraid I think, of falling asleep on top and falling off. About 4am we stopped at the edge of a small town, Nok Kundi, about 90 kilometers from the border. We were told this was to be a long stop.

We were the last to leave the bus. Exhausted, we dragged our rucksacks with us just a few yards from the vehicle and threw ourselves down at the side of the dirt road and slept on the hard baked earth. Peter and I were woken two or three hours later in the early morning light by the noise and activity around us.

We took soup and flatbread for breakfast from what passed for an open-air café in front of the border post, served by a silent turbaned Baluchi. We then made our way to the long, low mud-bricked building that passed as the border offices in this desolate place. Here we had our passports stamped for exiting Pakistan, even though we still had many more kilometers to travel to the Iranian border.

Back on the metal cooker we rattled on in increasing heat to the Pakistan border at Taftan. It was Friday and, having the usual stops for prayers, we arrived at the border about 3pm.

We crossed from the small, shabby, flat roofed, roughly built Pakistan office building where local tribespeople and border officials milled around in traditional dress. The officials were rough bearded with probably very limited education. Then the contrast of the modern and purpose built two-storey border offices in Iran where the officials were dressed in smart, dark green American style uniforms with polished boots, sunglasses and small black trimmed moustaches.

We needed to change money and just one black-market money changer was waiting for us on the Iranian side. The border security regarded him, it seemed, as the equivalent of a bank, for his fistfuls of US dollars and other currencies allowed us to change money into Rials for travel further into Iran. That Friday evening, we caught the local bus to Zahedan.

Chapter 18
To Zahedan

The modern Iranian road was tarmac smooth; of course it was. The fairly modern bus of Iranian make had suspensions and comfy seats but Peter was again on the roof-rack. Our Iranian fellow travellers were dressed in western clothing or robes with turbans and were therefore easily identifiable from the baggy trousered Baluchis.

We stopped early evening at a small village outside a mud-built mosque behind which the sun was declining. Change of country did not mean change of desert heat, and thirst at this time of the day seemed universal. In front of the mosque was a well, which the Baluchis and the Iranians began to use for refreshment. Along with all the other passengers I queued to take my turn as the large metal bowl, held by four chains, was let down into the well. The bowl was then raised for each to then drink from, and pour some cool water over their face or head. I watched carefully as I shuffled forward in the queue to see how to do it. As my

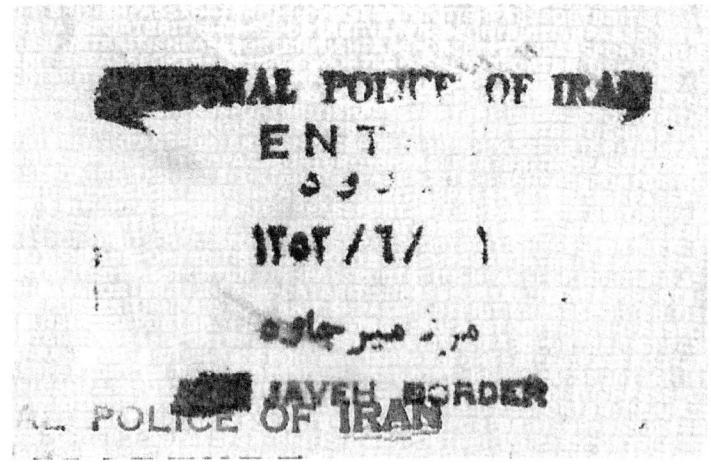

turn came up, I reached for the bowl. Suddenly, I found myself on the floor, felled from behind without pain or injury. There were loud voices and gesticulations amongst the men standing over me. Peter, who claimed allegiance to Islam and who had been able to drink freely ahead of me, explained. As a non-Muslim they would be very happy to let me drink from the well. But as an infidel I must not touch the bowl as the well was holy.

I was helped up by the men who had taken my legs from under me, and the bowl was let down and filled with water. As they held the bowl for me, I drank greedily and had some poured over my head. I thanked them greatly for their service. Smiles were all around.

Zahedan had modern concrete buildings; OK a bit brutalist, but three, four and five storeys high with glass in the windows and tarmacked roads and pavements. We arrived at the end of the day and bought baguettes of cheese and tomato and Pepsi from a bakery store; such a European meal after all my travels in foreign cuisine, and then we looked for a hotel for the night.

We were not going to find the cheap hippie hotels in this town, so far from the Silk Road. Two hotels claimed to be full, but I was becoming aware that the rooftops of each had human activity. At the third, we managed to persuade the manager that there must be room on the roof of his establishment, and he agreed.

Four floors up, as twilight fell and under a growing array of stars, were a score of beds laid in rows, mostly empty. The days may have been extremely hot but, as the sun disappeared, the air began to cool quickly, and I was grateful for my sleeping bag and the blanket that the hotelier gave to roof sleepers. It was an expensive night, yet refreshing too. Brits don't spend many nights being able to look up at a star filled sky and glittering Milky Way; UK nights are too cold and cloudy.

We woke up cold, with a view over the rooftops of this city to the outline of mountains around. Its streets below were quiet and ordered with clean, modern buildings, so different from the shabby, weathered, time-worn and walled structures of India, Pakistan and Afghanistan.

We bought our tickets for travel to Tehran by what passed for their national coach service and left that Saturday afternoon. In the evening we stopped at Kerman and changed coaches. We had to wait until early the next morning for the next coach to leave, and so with other Iranians we spread our sleeping bags or mats on the floor of the waiting room and slept until about 4am. We woke to much activity and joined the coach for the journey via Isfahan. Here Peter left us to visit the holy mosque, and I to journey on to Tehran.

Chapter 19
Tehran

I arrived in central Tehran about 2am on Monday morning. Getting down from the coach in the pitch dark I didn't recognise the area. My guess was that it was probably illegal to sleep rough in Tehran as the authorities would not want to encourage hippies to litter their streets.

Waiting for the other passengers to depart, I found a side street. Making sure I could not be seen from the main road, I curled up in the sleeping bag and, with my head on my rucksack, slept soundly in the alleyway. I was rudely awakened about 6am by the noise of workers calling and opening up the back doors of the shops and offices.

Uncertain of my bearings I took a taxi to the Central Post Office. There, at the Poste-Restante desk, I received four letters from home. My brother had promised to send me some money to a bank in Tehran. Great news! I found a seat on a bench in the middle of the busy post office. There was some relief in me that I had now rejoined the hippie trail from my detour to the south and the Post Restante desk was busy with hippies and travelers collecting mail. I closed my eyes from the heat and noise of hooting traffic outside and wanted to allow sleep to overtake me before I considered what to do next.

Just as I entered my doze, I was aware of someone taking a seat on the bench next to me. I inhaled a lady's perfume. Unwashed for more days than I liked to remember, I felt it only decent to move away and give her some room. I did so… and she moved too; and then a thigh moved against mine.

I opened my eyes and turned and met large, deep-shaded sunglasses on a young Iranian woman of perhaps thirty in a pretty, western-style, knee length print dress and just the flimsiest, flowered head-covering which she now moved back onto her shoulders. She smiled and slipped the sunglasses off. The skin was olive, the hair and eyes dark and the lips a softly painted red. The smile was quiet and intriguing.

Then the questions. 'Where have you come from?' 'How far have you travelled?' 'Did you get to India?' 'Oh, England, I love England.' Her thigh was still firmly against mine. 'I have been there with my husband a number of times.' She moved her head, and more perfume seeped towards me.

My interest in life was being renewed. Aryana (not her real name) beautiful, sensuous and in need of companionship and friendship was giving me all her attention. She continued to politely ignore my unwashed state. I was English and that was the top card in traveller conversations in Tehran. Her English was perfectly spoken and almost unaccented. Whatever my physical state, Aryana seemed to take pity on me and was persistent in wanting to show me the highlights of Tehran. How could I refuse?

Outside, she hailed a taxi, and we sat together on the back seat. The Muslim driver continually checked his mirror or turned around in the slow-moving traffic to view her beauty or to see if there was any impropriety. I think he hoped there was. Her head was now covered again, and the glasses stayed on, and I wondered if, out in the open with a western man, she preferred anonymity amongst her countrymen.

In the traffic, after a short journey, we became immobile, which embarrassed her. We pulled over and she instead insisted on taking me to the large Wimpy bar close to the gardens with the statue of the Shah.

She drew stares from other Iranian men enjoying their burgers and coke and kept her sunglasses on until we found a table with some privacy and ordered the food. She sat with her back to the crowd.

Aryana was lonely, even in the country of her birth. She had lived from a young child with her parents in the Netherlands where her father had been in business. There she had fallen in love and married young, to a Dutchman. But after ten years had recently become divorced. It was easy to see that her life in western Europe had given her dreams and hopes for a western-style life which even the modernizing of the Shah's Iran could not satisfy.

At some point she had lived with her husband in London, and she hated this life in Tehran with its still conservative religious expectations, social restrictions and its poor imitation of western life and freedoms. Where else in all Persia could an Iranian woman spontaneously start a conversation with a single man, except in the confines of the Post Office by the Poste-Restante desk surrounded by westerners.

In the years that followed I wondered if Aryana had escaped and survived the Islamic Revolution of 1979 that swept aside people like her, and imprisoned or executed them for their decadent or western lifestyle. Many years later, I found her online. Aryana is the name I have given her; but she had given me her real first and family names. She had married again and, seeing the revolution coming, had found sanctuary back in Europe where she lived and worked as an artist.

It was time to collect my brother's money. It would have been so much easier if he had just put some dollars or pound notes in an envelope for me. But Barclays Bank in England had sent the money to a bank in Tehran, but his letter gave me no idea which bank. Unlike in the UK, where there were only four banks in any high street at that time (Barclays, NatWest, Midland and Lloyds) in this city, as in India, there were literally dozens of banks of different names.

I went into the first and spoke to the clerk at the counter labelled, *Foreign Exchange*. He invited me up the wide, marbled staircase to a floor filled with men all sat at large desks which were all covered in paper. I sat at his desk as he looked through the paperwork that was piled in front of him. Computers were going to make their lives so much easier. He said they did not have my money.

By the fourth bank I gave up. The money was here in Tehran somewhere, but it was not for me to know. Disappointed, I knew I was going to need to tighten my belt just a little more for the next few days. Once back in Istanbul, Magic Bus should be waiting for me.

Sleeping out was going to be much cooler than in any hotel. But I was unwilling to risk a night out again and the public parks were so full of people staying out of the buildings in the heat. I found a cheap hotel called Toos. There were several hippies and travellers in the courtyard as well as a group of smart, young, educated Iranian men who were keen to explore their English and to try their luck to impress the English girl travellers.

The next day was frustrating as I would have to wait until the evening for the Mihan coach to Erzerum. Would I be in Erzerum in time for the evening train to Istanbul? I had

شرکت مسافربری و حمل و قل بین المللی میهن تور		Ticket No. شماره بلیط
MIHAN TOUR CO. LTD. International Travel & Transport		№ 08386
Amount مبلغ 7-50	From: مبدأ OMAN	Dep.Time ساعت حرکت 7 PM
Sig & Stamp. امضاء ومهر شرکت	To: مقصد ERZERUM	Dep.Date تاریخ حرکت 27-8
	Passenger Name and Address نام مسافر و آدرس قیمت	

banked on a morning coach departure, yet I should still be on target for timely arrival in Istanbul on Saturday. How to spend the day? Forget the banks for my brother's money. It was time to lighten my load.

I had carried a small one-man tent in my rucksack, you may remember. It was never used. The hotels were so cheap, and the nights had been warm for sleeping out so far. Magic Bus was just five days away. No need to keep it and any money, admittedly it would be in Iranian Rials, would still be useful. I spent the morning hawking it around a few of the small, daily-produce shops, whose owners mostly spoke some English, to no avail. In my search for a new owner, I wandered into an area of the city where the roads, backstreets and alleyways were filled with car and bicycle repair shops. A few owners gave me a shake of the head, but one owner, who was standing by the door of his spare-part supplies shop in a state of boredom waiting for custom, was curiously observing me as I made my way up the alley.

He was unenthusiastic about my offer. Maybe that was his bartering technique. But he hadn't outright refused me as the others had done. So, a little more persistence from me was needed. I then offered to put the tent up for him. He demurred, pursed his lips and then let me through to his back yard. A few minutes later I left with some useful Rials in my pocket for food for the onward journey.

At 7pm Tuesday 27th I left by Mihan Tour coach from Tehran and arrived about the same time on Wednesday at Erzerum in eastern Turkey, the shantytown city. A good speedy trip that kept up with my timetable made three weeks back in Bombay. But sadly, I was just too late to catch the evening train to Istanbul.

You can guess my disappointment. It was not simply that I would have to spend another night in a hotel, I had the money for that. Now time was tight, and I needed no more travel interruptions if I was to be back in Istanbul to catch the Magic Bus next Sunday morning. Every day now was precious. If I missed that bus I would need every penny I had.

Erzurum in August was like a November day in England for snow was still on top of the surrounding peaks and I was, of course, dressed in light clothes for the summer heat that was now well gone. I had no autumn or winter clothing and with the flesh I had lost in India, I was freezing.

I spent the night in a small and otherwise empty hotel. All the next day I wandered the streets and alleyways, always being sure of my bearings, to kill time until the train arrived. When the cold became too much I used cafés to keep warm. A diary I had started to write, I somehow lost here.

Chapter 20
Greek Border Crisis

At 6pm on Thursday I boarded the slow 'Erzerum Express' train that again made all the stops and sluggishly arrived in Istanbul on Saturday evening, 31st August. The first Sunday of the month was tomorrow and the Magic Bus should have arrived by now to leave in the morning. The Hotel Gungor near to the Pudding Shop café, was the pick-up point. But outside the café and the hotel that evening there was no sign of the coach amongst the colourful and eclectic mix of other vehicles.

I asked the customers in the Pudding Shop. But they were distracted by other events. What people were talking about was the invasion of the island of Cyprus by Turkish forces. Turkey claimed they were trying to protect the Turkish nationals on the island from the Greeks.

This war had begun when I was in India, and to which a month ago I showed no interest at all. Surely it couldn't be that serious. It had merited only a small paragraph on page five of the Times of India. But had I returned via the hippie trail rather than through Quetta and Zahedan, news of this event and its effect on us hippie trail travellers would have reached me before now.

The fighting part of this war was over but there was no peace yet. Hippies at the tables were talking about problems getting across the Turkish border with Greece. Was it closed or open now? Was it closed to vehicles, but walkers could get through? Were train services running? None seemed sure.

What was true was that the hotels were getting practically no trade over the last month from those heading east to India. And the number of those heading back to the UK was growing each day. Many, by this time, were running short of money, holed up in Istanbul. Indeed, as you remember, my ticket home on Magic Bus had been my insurance policy from the start. I thought I had been clever. Now the Magic Bus had either been turned back at the border or decided that travel through Greece and Turkey was not advisable due to the war. Maybe it had never left Belgium.

Sunken feelings of disappointment and anger enveloped me. And a real frustration at what to do next. In the days of no social media, getting instant news of which crossings might be open at any time was simply not possible and was hugely frustrating.

'If the border's closed, you gotta go back through Bulgaria by train, man,' said a dude behind his black moustache and sunglasses.

'We haven't got the money for that,' a girl at a table next to me called across.

'Then get to the Consulate and get them to cable your family to send the money through,' came the reply. 'If family haven't got the money to send you, the Consulate can still repatriate you.'

'Nah,' said her companion. 'Someone said they're lettin' the walkers through but not the vehicles. If we can get across, we can hitch up through Greece and get back home that way. Maybe a week to do it. We should be OK.'

How much money did I have? If no Magic Bus then, was hitching back through Europe or the train through Bulgaria my only options? Magic Bus may arrive tomorrow, but that looked to be an increasingly unlikely proposition. Could I afford to wait to see if it would arrive later in the week, or next Saturday? If it doesn't arrive I will have wasted days here and precious money too. Did I have the £30GB for the train through Bulgaria? I would also need to buy a visa for that.

I had to do some serious thinking, and on later reflection I don't think I made the best choice.

I determined that wasn't going to the British Consulate and get them to contact my family for the train ride. I reckoned that if I was careful I could have enough money on me to keep me afloat while I hitched up through Europe. The Magic Bus had only taken three days to get here. Therefore, I could get to the border and try and cross by foot and then chance my luck in thumbing lifts back to the UK.

'Sell your blood for $10 a pint at one of the Athens hospitals,' another guy chipped in, as the conversation on this group of tables developed. I had heard that kind of story before - Meshad. Swans can break your arm, but no-one knows of anyone it has happened to.

I had enough money for another night in a hotel, found a bank to cash some more and then the next day, Tuesday, I checked at the Gungor Hotel. No, the Magic Bus had not arrived. They had had no news of it. It was never late. It should have been here days ago. They did not believe it would be turning up now.

I took the local bus to a less frequented border crossing at Edirne that some thought might be a better bet for a foot crossing. I had no success in hitching a ride to the border. No westerners were heading that way, of course. After a long afternoon on a bus, I arrived at the Turkish border in the evening about 6pm. The Turks confirmed that their border was open. They gave me a cursory glance, stamped my passport and let me pass through.

A quarter of a mile walk through no-man's-land down a short, wooded country road led to the Greek border post made up of an office building and a road barrier. A company of Greek soldiers looked in relaxed mood. The border was open, the official advised me, as I waited at his desk for him to stamp my passport. I appeared to be their only customer. Indeed, a crossing not much used. He stamped it. To my great relief I was through!

The worst of the Turkish war with the Greeks on Cyprus may have been over, but not the politics. One Greek took a different view from his border colleague of this weary and unwashed, hippie traveller, rough-bearded and alone. As I look back I can see that I had all the appearance of a social outcast, and should not have been surprised that an army officer standing close by eyed me suspiciously. As the official handed me back my passport, he snatched it from his hand and examined it flicking through the pages irritably. He frowned and indicated to me to follow him and, as he led me outside and down the wooden steps of the building, he called over to the group of soldiers.

Then he turned to me and rubbed his moustache as his troops gathered round. His mood was grim. But his troops were beginning to grin.

'How much money you got?' he demanded. To pass through Greece I legally needed £30 or equivalent.

'Plenty,' I said, hoping that my boastful confidence might help them overlook my unkempt appearance and grubby, sweat-stained clothes.

'How much? Let me see it,' he persisted, holding out his hand as if to take my money bag from me.

'Well… a lot of it is in foreign currency,' I stalled trying to sound confidant. 'I've got Indian and Iranian, and other countries' money including European and US dollars.'

'Show me,' he snapped his fingers and thrust out his hand.

I slowly pulled out my, by now, dirty and stained, somewhat crumpled leather wallet from beneath my shirt and emptied out all the money I had. He could have taken a generous view of my coins and paper money; but my collection of left-over Rials, Afghanis, Paise and Rupees from the countries I had travelled through was not a fortune. Not even the small collection of US dollars convinced him that it could add up to the equivalent of GB£30. (Equivalent to about £250 today.)

'You do not have enough money to come through Greece,' he sneered. His soldiers pressed in and agreed with him, smiling mockingly as they did so. Then the truth came out.

'You bloody British. Your bloody Mr Callaghan. Why he take side with the Turks? Eh? Greece is friend of Britain, not bloody Turks!' The officer was angry.

I knew nothing about the Turkish/Greek war or what part Britain and its Labour prime minister had played in it. Weeks ago, I had been stoned by Rajasthan youths for my government's even-handedness with the Indians and the Pakistanis over the war that created Bangladesh. Now the Greeks were angry with me over their Cyprus war with Turkey. Did I say at the beginning of this book that it was easy to travel the hippie trail as a Brit? Countries may not have wanted me to pay for visas, but my government's foreign policies were costing me dear.

'You not coming through,' the officer snapped, and he

scrumbled through my passport to find the page and scribbled a note underneath the official's stamp.

Back at the Turkish side the official took my passport, crossed out the exit stamp, and sent me to walk back along the road to the Turkish town. I slept under a copse of trees with only the comfort of another cloudless night with the Milky Way silently circling above me. The next day I caught the bus back to Istanbul.

Chapter 21
Sultanahmet

It was late afternoon when I arrived back to Istanbul. In a dejected state I crossed the bridge and made my way up the hill to the British Consulate; a large building with iron gates, thankfully still open. This was the only option left for me now.

I explained my position to the man at the door. He let me through to a room with a counter at the far end. I was not alone. Several other hippies and travellers were in the same predicament. With the Greek border difficult to negotiate, the only other guaranteed way back to the UK was now by rail on the Orient Express through Bulgaria, Yugoslavia, Italy and France and then ferry to the UK. An expensive £30 journey.

It was close to closing time, but the Turkish lady took my details.

'Do you need repatriating?' she asked evenly, eying my unkempt state through her spectacles.

'No,' I said, 'I just need my family in the UK to be contacted to send my money through.'

'If you are repatriated it will be written into your passport and you will be required to repay it when back in the UK. You won't be allowed to go abroad again until it is repaid.' She had said this sentence many times recently, I guessed.

'I don't need government money, thank you,' I said, getting a little exasperated. 'I just need a phone call to my family in the UK to send the money for the train through Bulgaria.' I showed her my passport and the comment of the Greek border officer.

She looked at me over her specs. 'The Orient Express through Bulgaria is the only way you can get back to the

UK now the border with Greece is closed. That or fly. Give me the details of your family in the UK. We will contact them, and they can send us the money for you. It will take about a week to all come through.'

She said to call back the next day, and surprised me with the offer of a loan of some money to see me through the next twenty-four hours. I was playing safe now. I took it.

With the uncertainty of the week ahead, I decided not to sleep in one of the Sultanahmet hotels for that night. The weather was still intense and sleeping out with a sleeping bag would be no problem. I had come to enjoy the warm nights and the peace of the starry hosts above. Besides, listening to travellers' tales in the Pudding Shop was becoming repetitive and depressing.

The Sultanahmet district of Istanbul is much changed now, but at that time the area to the side and back of the Blue Mosque was rough, unkempt ground with trees, shrubs and bushes. It was therefore easy enough, once the street traders had gone, the shops and cafés had closed and darkness had descended, to find a place to sleep as comfortably as I could.

The next day the Consulate offered to loan me money for each day of the week, which would be repaid when my money came through. The lady asked me which hotel I was going to book myself into. I told her. She looked at me and with no indication of emotion said, 'We took a body out of there three weeks ago. Overdose. Flew it back home to his family in the UK.'

The hippie hotel cost me 10TL for a shared room. By Friday the money would come; I was happy for my family to raid my savings account. I would need £40 - which was enough for the train and £10 for the money the Consulate had loaned me for daily expenses.

The week of waiting around Sultanahmet seemed to be

forever. I passed the time in visiting the Bazaar and in the cafés or the park sitting, people-watching, talking and sharing stories with those few heading out to, or the many coming back from Kabul, Nepal or India.

The hotel beds were bare board with the thinnest of mattresses and the 10TL allowed you to come and go during the day. I shared the room with a young hippie of dark Mediterranean looks, yet his nationality could only be guessed at. Shoulder-length black hair and unkempt beard, he spoke to no-one, and avoided eye contact with everyone.

On his bed or walking in the street he had a huge ghetto-blaster on his shoulder with large grey, wired earphones glued to the side of his head and a sack of rock-music tapes hanging from his belt.

Mostly he lay on his bed in our room and when his eyes weren't closed he focused on nothing, staring blankly ahead or at the ceiling, with the faint sound of rock bands emitting from the headphones. He responded to no question or comment. His movements were limited to his eating habits which were to reach into a paper bag of nuts he had bought at one of the street stalls, and consistently chew. He ate nothing else.

Once when I came into the room, he was changing his shirt. I had worked with homeless men in the UK, and when I saw the hundreds of black spots all over his back, I recognized the sure sign of scabies. His obsessions didn't stretch to keeping his body clean. Heaven help the hippie who would lie in the bed after him. Some said he came from a rich family and that he could afford to stay in Sultanahmet as long as he liked.

Getting myself a shish-kebab one evening from a stall in the street I met Martin and Rob. They were interested in the overland public transport journey to India and so they invited me back to their shared room in a hotel up near the Bazaar. We ate the food we had bought, and I gave them what information I could about the trail.

The evening was darkening as Rob drew out a candle and set it up on the floor in front of us. However, this was not to be a meditation or focus for prayer to any of the religious deities to be encountered on the hippie trail. For a length of rubber hose appeared and then a dessert spoon.

Rob's eyes were bright now in the candlelight and, a little breathless, he reached into his rucksack and drew out a bottle with a label that looked like it had come from a chemist. It had.

He proceeded with an unsteady hand to pour some of the liquid onto the spoon. He looked up at me, pleased with his efforts so far, and slowly moved the spoon over the flickering flame.

'Stuff's got morphine in it. Got it from the chemist,'

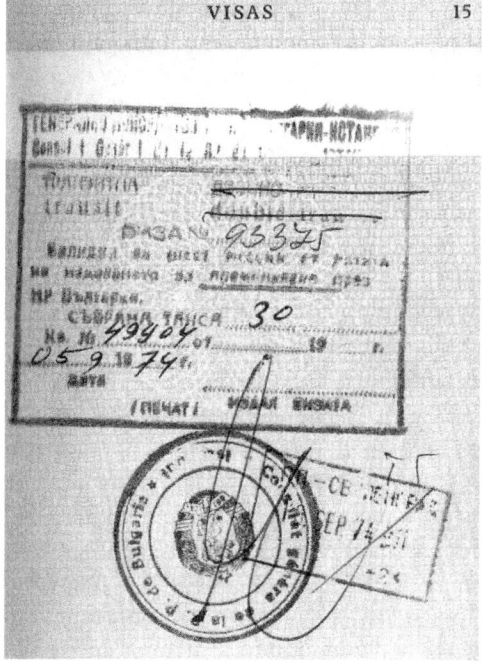

Martin explained. 'Rob's goin' to burn off the impurities and then we inject the stuff. You get a great high! Have a turn in a minute.' I declined his offer, which I was sure was generously meant.

Rob had loaded up the syringe and was tightening the rubber cord around his upper arm. 'What are you going to do when you get back to England,' he asked.

'I'm going to train to be a social worker,' I said.

They both looked up at me in genuine surprise. Martin laughed and shrugged. 'Fuck me,' he said, 'I'm going to India to get away from mine!'

I found a second-hand shop in Sultanahmet and sold my red rucksack. I simply wanted to lighten my load and any more money would be useful. The shopkeeper eyed me curiously. He was getting a lot of stuff pushed his way by hippies and travellers on the return journey. His problem was that nobody was coming through to buy from him for their journey to India. His price was low, but I wasn't arguing with him. He offered me a cotton bag, and for the few possessions I now had, that was all I needed.

On Friday I visited the Consulate again and they gave me the money from home. I now needed to get to the Bulgarian Embassy to buy the visa to travel by train through the country, tonight. A shared taxi ride with two others in the same predicament took us to a smart two-story building in one of the suburbs. I paid the visa fee, and the Bulgarian Embassy official stamped the passport.

It was here I met Gary and he joined us for the taxi ride back into the centre of the city. He too planned to be on the train, but he asked me for money for food. So, we made our way into a café where he told me his story.

Gary, tall and broad without much meat on his frame, had been in an Afghan prison for two years for possessing drugs, too many drugs for the authorities to ignore, I guessed. He had been buying it from a farmer who came to the market, and Gary made a deal with him in the hope of making some money in selling it on to the hippies. Gary was to be the middleman in what he thought would be a nice little operation where no one could get hurt and he could make a comfortable living in a lifestyle he enjoyed.

But a police raid on the market had given him two years in jail. He was still angry and resentful at this, in a country that, at that time, had such a reputation for selling hashish and opium freely. Gary was depressed, not making much eye contact, and probably was still in a state of shock as to what had happened to him. A hippie who has just experienced two years without drugs, sex, rock music, companionship and news of western life would have been emotionally and environmentally deprived, without the additional privations of an Afghan prison.

In prison Gary had had to pay for his own food to be brought in by the family of one of the guards. His sister in the UK had sent him money to a Kabul bank so he could pay the people to do this for him. Now he was on his way back to the UK in something of an unhappy state. We separated to collect our respective bags and arranged to meet at the rail station later and travel back to the UK together.

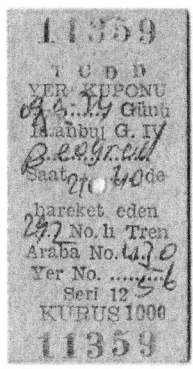

Chapter 22
The Orient Express

By 6pm I had walked down from Sultanahmet to the Sirkici railway station for the departure of the Orient Express. At the far end of Platform One stood a massive monster of a continental steam engine, clanging and releasing geysers of white steam far in front of the dark blue, high coaches that I climbed up into. A corridor ran aside the compartments and the universal train smells of steam and dust and human bodies perfumed the air. I found a place in a shabby compartment with wooden bench seats. There was little luxury in this part of the Orient Express.

I had checked the platform for Gary. There was no sign of him and watching from the carriage window he failed to appear before we left. I could have done with the company, and wondered at what reason he might have found not to travel, having already got his visa for Bulgaria. Maybe someone had offered him a joint.

A long, loud trumpet call from the engine and at 8pm the train screeched, the carriages jolted and slowly rolled, and I let out a huge sigh of relief. The final journey home from Asia had begun.

A little after 9pm the guard, in time-worn dark blue trousers and jacket, came in and in a grumpy manner demanded the blinds be drawn down. The train would soon be coming up to the Bulgarian border whose communist government was extremely cautious about what outsiders might see from the carriage windows. Hence the train could only travel through the country at night.

That night was spent dozing on the benches with two other Turks, and by morning the guard appeared again. The blinds were up, and we were in the sunlight of rural Yugoslavia, chuffing past scenes from rural Victorian England.

Dilapidated small, farm buildings with outdated machinery drawn by patient shire horses or oxen across fields high now with corn; and stone and gravel roads where horses pulled hay wagons and carts. Not even a steam engine, a common site from Victorian England through to the Second World War and beyond, was seen to ease their load. The people had no curiosity for the train as we sped through, but a girl suddenly looked up from leading a cow into a field for milking, and then she was gone.

In Belgrade we changed trains for the Italian border, and I met up with another traveller, David, who had also been trapped in Istanbul by the war with the Greeks. Coming out of the Communist Block of countries, a new train took us through Venice, and we caught sight of the Doge's Palace across the waters. Then, as the evening drew on, we passed the Alps and through the night sped up through France until we arrived in Paris at about 10am the following morning. A hurried change of trains again and we were on our way to Calais.

The trip across the channel was rough. Yet the sight of the iconic white cliffs was unexpectedly emotional. Those cliffs, that had welcomed most Brits from their foreign trips before the advent of air-travel, were reassuring evidence of 'home'. England, or now more accurately Great Britain, was that *'precious stone set in a silver sea'* as Shakespeare made one of his characters proclaim. After the browns, khakis, yellows and dark greens of Asian travel, I had a psychological hunger for the soft nourishing greens of the English landscape and the cool, fresh, rain-filtered air of home.

In Dover, with the passport controls behind us, I caught the train to London arriving late afternoon on Monday, in time for the final journey to Bristol.

Chapter 23
Magic Bus Again

A few days later, I called the phone number on the Magic Bus card. I wanted some money back. A woman came on the line and agreed very reluctantly to meet me a few days later at their new offices in the Holloway Road, North London.

'No, you can't have a refund. We don't do refunds.' She was adamant.

'I have paid for a service you have not supplied,' I responded. I knew the law. 'Did you send the coach out to Turkey in September at the end of the fighting part of the war?'

OK, she admitted, they had not bothered to send the coach because of the problems they guessed there would still be at the borders.

'But you left your paying customers stranded. You didn't fulfill the terms of the contract we had with you,' I said.

If they had made the journey and been turned back at the border that would have been fine for me. They could have kept my money. But they hadn't even spent my money on the journey, and had had no thought for the travellers who would have been depending on them for the return to the UK.

I demanded a refund of half the money. The return trip money. She said, 'No'.

I said, 'Your Magic Bus is well named. It can completely disappear when you least expect it. I'll take you to the Small Claims Court.'

I got their cheque for £22.50 in the post two days later day.

Epilogue

Those of us who had travelled the 'hippie trail' to India from the 1950s to the 70s, may well have had a sense of reflection over the intervening years about who we were then and who we are now as, in the 3rd decade of the 21st century, we become more sensitized to ethnic and cultural differences in our own countries.

The hippie trail was off the tourist maps of the great middle classes in the countries from which we all came. These Middle Eastern states, at that time, did not experience middle class westerners with their wealth staying in top hotels and bringing in much needed money to their shopkeepers and revenues to their governments. This white, mobile community of western youth scraped money together to make the trip, and maybe we were not the best example of what the First World nations had to offer the people of the countries we visited.

At times, whether hippies or not, did we present ourselves as largely ignorant and insensitive to cultural differences? The few printed guides gave very little information on any of the social expectations of the Muslim or Hindu cultures, and any offence that might be caused by differences of dress, presentation or appearance. Did our western European and American whiteness give us a sense of entitlement and privilege that could at times be both condescending and racist, judged by today's values?

Did we mock the attempts of Iran to modernise itself and create a consumer culture? Did we not understand that the baggy trousers and long shirts of the Afghan men and the loose-fitting clothing of Muslim women was to hide any indication of their sexuality, and that the tight or revealing clothing of our men and women would be offensive to them? The freedoms that the hippy trail travellers expressed should still have come with personal responsibilities. Tourists today take great care not to offend the peoples of the countries they visit.

My own motives for travelling I have explained, and I met plenty of travellers for whom the adventure of the journey was enough. We didn't all need drugs to enhance the experience, and for some they clouded it.

Perhaps most westerners on the trail, without much thought, involved themselves in some small way at least, with the drug trade in the countries they passed through. Those who indulged in buying marijuana/hashish/opium must have, in some very small part, encouraged the growth of that country's drug trade amongst its own youth, from Turkey to India and Nepal. The growing of hashish and opium poppies had always been part of rural farming in some parts of Afghanistan. Yet the activities of hippies must have encouraged this fledgling industry, that continued for the next fifty years to wreak havoc in the lives of westerners through the smuggling of drugs into Europe, even after the borders with these countries were closed by war or revolution.

Nor did the fledgling ideas of socialism appeal to these western travellers. They found the increasing restrictions on the availability of drugs in Afghanistan, from 1974 onwards under an increasingly Soviet socialist influence, irksome to their own needs.

British people up to the Thatcher era of the 1980s would never complain about poor service or shoddy workmanship for fear of embarrassing themselves. Let's face it, for years we made some of the world's worst cars and kept on buying them; remember the Hillman Imp or the Austin Allegro?

We had neither the temperament nor the skills of bartering or haggling that were the preferred method of sales in bazaars or market stalls. We hippie trail travellers maybe too often talked of being 'ripped off' and paying too much, when all we did was lack the verbal skills, self-confidence and cultural awareness of buying and selling in Middle Eastern nations.

As travellers we stood out, particularly in the more conservative Muslim countries, for what they saw as our hedonism and free-living lifestyles. Many have asked the question before; had we been the example of western values that finally persuaded the people of Iran to call in the 1979 Islamic Revolution? Had we helped Afghanistan lose its king to be replaced by increasingly more conservative, socialist idealists and finally the rigid anti-western religious zeal of the Taliban? Pakistan too. These three neighbours, on the ancient Silk Road to the East, so hospitable to the hippies at one level, refused ultimately to accept their western values of independent thought, travel and ideas.

And so were we, as hippy trail travellers, the kind of uninvited guests at the neighbour's party, who offended the hosts by our loud behaviour and drinking too much, and then complained about the party food and entertainment. Were we then sick in their garden? Many of us were not that clever. We were not the best that the West could offer those countries, and perhaps the only saving grace was that we didn't abuse their women.

It was a different world then, and we, as white westerners, had different values ourselves. As our own countries have become more ethnically diverse through immigration, most of us have become more sensitive to other people's ethnicity and cultures.

For all of us, the hippie trail was an adventure. You didn't always know exactly what you would find in the next village, town or city. The countries we travelled through were not geared for tourists as we know it today. Their religions and cultural values that had set in place their laws, customs and traditions could be quite different to ours. The lack of guidebooks and tourist facilities meant we lived a life much closer to the people whose nations we passed through. We ate the food of the ordinary people and slept in beds of the simplest make.

Sometimes oyster and sometimes lobster; I had had a bit of an adventure myself. Stoned (with rocks) in Rajasthan, assaulted in southern Iran, refused entry to Greece, slept rough on the streets of Tehran and Istanbul; but can claim to have dined at the Pudding Shop in Sultanahmet and at Siggi's in Kabul; travelled down the Khyber Pass, crossed deserts, sampled Muslim and Hindu cultures and did get to the heart of India and back. And in the years of secretive communist governments, I travelled on the 'mysterious' Orient Express from Istanbul to Paris.

We take for granted the daily shower, the turn of the tap for water to drink, the fridge keeping our foods fresh and cool; air conditioning in the home, office and cars; and knowing that in Europe now, Health and Safety legislation keeps us safe at all times.

On our journeys east, we had a lot of fun and adventure. We sought and found a wide range of new experiences and perhaps learned a lot about ourselves in the process. Maybe too, we made some friends for life.

Thirty years later and our daughter, like many of her generation, took a six-month trip to Australia and New Zealand. She even bumped into a school friend who, unknown to her, had got a job working in the restaurant on top of the Sky Tower in Auckland. A much safer trip. Would we as parents today have sanctioned our young adult children going on the hippie trail in the 1970s?

Looking back, we can perhaps see that many of us took risks and were unprepared for what we found. Each day took us on uncertain transport to a new country, town or village, to sleep in hotels, bug ridden or not, to eat uncertain food we trusted to be OK from wayside cafés and market stalls, with not too much idea of what we would find at our next destination. We travelled with a hotch-potch of other westerners by no means all signed-up hippies, with whom we made fleeting relationships.

But I would also like to record how grateful I was to have seen and experienced the friendliness of Muslim, Hindu and Christian peoples, throughout this journey, who offered respect, friendship, hospitality, kindness and a generosity of spirit to me as a foreign traveller in their lands.

They say Magellan was the world's greatest explorer, not Neil Armstrong. Magellan never knew from day to day what he would see and find in the first circumnavigation of the world. Neil Armstrong had a pretty good idea what he would see and find on the Moon. He just had to get there.

Did I ever go back, as I had hoped to, and do the trip again as a tourist, with a camera when I had a bit more cash and could travel in a bit more comfort? No. Time, life and international politics defeated me on that one.

We were young and, hippie or not, we were all brave adventurers, and if you had a few weeks or months on your hands, living and travelling in Asia could be done at our own pace and was extremely cheap. But never again in my lifetime will I, or my children in their lifetimes, be able to travel in and through those countries so freely, cheaply and so safely as we did in those days when the land route to India was known as the Hippie Trail.

And finally: What of Mr Ahmellah? It wasn't that I hadn't looked for a commercial dictionary as he had requested when I met him in Kandahar. But the enormous size of them and postage charges discouraged me. However, walking down Christmas Steps in Bristol the following Spring, I explored George's secondhand bookshop. Here to my delight, I found a smaller pocket-sized commercial dictionary that looked the kind to post safely to Afghanistan. At the post office there was much searching through leaflets to decide the amount of postage needed and interested questions from the post-lady behind the counter.

I put my address inside the thick envelope in case he wanted to respond. Also, a reply from him would give me some clue that it had arrived safely. I got no reply. Maybe he had received by post many commercial dictionaries from the other travellers he had met.

Note
As I have not wanted to embarrass any of the amazing and extraordinary characters that I met on the trail, I have changed many names of people in writing this book.

Printed in Great Britain
by Amazon